A Reasonable Christian Faith

A Reasonable Christian Faith

DANIEL RALPH KERN

WIPF & STOCK · Eugene, Oregon

A REASONABLE CHRISTIAN FAITH

Copyright © 2022 Daniel Ralph Kern. All rights reserved. Except for brief quotations in critical publications or reviews, no part of this book may be reproduced in any manner without prior written permission from the publisher. Write: Permissions, Wipf and Stock Publishers, 199 W. 8th Ave., Suite 3, Eugene, OR 97401.

Wipf & Stock
An Imprint of Wipf and Stock Publishers
199 W. 8th Ave., Suite 3
Eugene, OR 97401

www.wipfandstock.com

PAPERBACK ISBN: 978-1-6667-4384-5
HARDCOVER ISBN: 978-1-6667-4385-2
EBOOK ISBN: 978-1-6667-4386-9

OCTOBER 3, 2022 12:20 PM

The Scriptures quoted are from the NET Bible® https://netbible.com copyright ©1996, 2019 used with permission from Biblical Studies Press, L.L.C. All rights reserved.

Contents

Dedication | vii

Introduction | ix

Part 1: The *Concept* of a Reasonable Christian Faith | 1
    A *Reasonable* Christian Faith | 1
    A Reasonable *Christian* Faith | 29
    A Reasonable Christian *Faith* | 36

Part 2: The *Content* of a Reasonable Christian Faith | 40
    The Two Images of God | 40
    What is God Like? | 41
    What does God want from us? | 52
    Jesus and the Rest of the Bible | 84

Part 3: *Applications* of a Reasonable Christian Faith | 87
    The LGBTQIA+ Community | 87

Part 4: *Challenges* to a Reasonable Christian Faith | 93
    The Absence of God | 93
    Why the World Is the Way It Is | 94
    Pain and Suffering | 95

Conclusion | 103

Bibliography | 105

Dedication

THIS BOOK IS DEDICATED to my children, Danielle and Henry. Being responsible for their well-being has radically changed my view of God. As they grow up in this complicated world, if my thoughts can be of any guidance to them, I will be satisfied.

The book is also dedicated to the Philosophy Club at Chaffey College. As the faculty advisor for the Philosophy Club for the past 15 years, I have had many deep and engaging discussions with my students about the relationship between faith and reason. I have found them to be eager, concerned, people grappling with one of life's fundamental questions. If anything I say here can help anyone with this question, I will be very happy.

Introduction

Religion, particularly Christianity, has a bad rap. One of the primary attackers is a group of thinkers known as "The New Atheists"—Sam Harris, Christopher Hitchens, Richard Dawkins, and Daniel Dennett. The titles of their books are instructive: *The End of Faith* (Harris), *God is Not Great* (Hitchens), *The God Delusion* (Dawkins), *Breaking the Spell: Religion as a Natural Phenomenon* (Dennett). Here are some of the things they say about religion:

> Where I think we disagree is on the nature of faith itself. I think that faith is, in principle, in conflict with reason (and, therefore, that religion is necessarily in conflict with science) ... My use of the word is meant to capture belief in specific religious propositions without sufficient evidence—prayer can heal the sick, there is a supreme Being listening to our thoughts, we will be reunited with our loved ones after death, etc.... Given my view of faith, I think that [even] religious "moderation" is basically an elaborate exercise in self-deception.[1]

> Our belief is not a belief. Our principles are not a faith. We do not rely solely upon science and reason, because these are necessary rather than sufficient factors, but we distrust anything that contradicts science or outrages reason. We may differ on many things, but what we respect is free inquiry, openmindedness, and the pursuit of ideas for their own sake ... Violent, irrational, intolerant, allied to racism and tribalism and bigotry, invested

---

1. Harris, "Is Religion Built upon Lies?"

Introduction

in ignorance and hostile to free inquiry, contemptuous of women and coercive toward children: organized religion ought to have a great deal on its conscience.[2]

The take-home message is that we should blame religion itself, not religious extremism—as though that were some kind of terrible perversion of real, decent religion. Voltaire got it right long ago: 'Those who can make you believe absurdities can make you commit atrocities.' So did Bertrand Russell: 'Many people would sooner die than think. In fact, they do.'[3]

I should emphasize this, to keep well-meaning but misguided multiculturalists at bay: the theoretical entities in which these tribal people frankly believe — the gods and other spirits—don't exist. These people are mistaken, and you know it as well as I do. It is possible for highly intelligent people to have a very useful but mistaken theory, and we don't have to pretend otherwise in order to show respect for these people and their ways.[4]

The New Atheist arguments are more than 10 years old. To show that anti-religion sentiment is not dead, this is from a recent opinion article in the New York Times:

> God, it seems, paints with a wide brush. He paints with a roller. In Egypt, said our rabbi, he even killed firstborn cattle. He killed cows. If he were mortal, the God of Jews, Christians and Muslims would be dragged to The Hague. And yet we praise him. We emulate him. We implore our children to be like him.
>
> Perhaps now, as missiles rain down and the dead are discovered in mass graves, is a good time to stop emulating this hateful God. Perhaps we can stop extolling his brutality. Perhaps now is a good time to teach our children to pass over God—to be as unlike him as possible[5]

2. Hitchens, *God Is Not Great*, 5.
3. Dawkins, *The God Delusion*, 306.
4. Dennett, *Religion as a Natural Phenomenon*, 409.
5. Auslander, "In This Time of War, I Propose We Give Up God."

Introduction

Religion, according to these commentators, is, in a word, bad. The main reasons for that are that it is based on faith, which puts it in conflict with reason and science, and that God has a bad character. My main purpose in this book is to argue that both claims are wrong. I agree with them that many religious people throughout history have acted on a faith that was irrational, in conflict with reason and science, and which led (and continues to lead) them to commit horrible atrocities in the name of that faith, and that the God portrayed by religious people often has a bad character. But I will argue that it is not inherent to religious faith to be irrational or lead to atrocities. In fact, I will argue that the nature of (Christian) religion and faith does *not* to lead to these results, and that anyone acting in these ways is failing to be religious or faithful. The New Atheists are throwing the baby out with the bathwater.

I am not setting out to "prove" anything, in the style of traditional apologetics. I simply plan to make a case that it is reasonable to have faith that a good, loving, God exists.

Part 1

The *Concept* of a Reasonable Christian Faith

A *REASONABLE* CHRISTIAN FAITH

THE OXFORD ENGLISH DICTIONARY defines "reason" as "the power of the mind to think and form valid judgements by a process of logic."[1] In my own logic courses and textbooks, I define reason as "the ability to come to a conclusion based on the evaluation of evidence." Reason is a power or an ability that humans (and some animals) have to evaluate evidence and form judgments or come to conclusions. Reason is a fundamental aspect of human existence. It has been taken throughout history as the most characteristic and unique feature of humans.[2]

An interesting question about reason is what role it should play in human decision-making. Typically, reason has been set against emotions or passions as the two most basic influences in

---

1. http://www.oed.com/view/Entry/159068?rskey=8Y84kb&result=1#eid.
2. Many people, maybe most people, now take it that some animals have reason as well, and there seems to be good evidence for this fact. However, no animals that we know of have reason at remotely the same level as humans, so it is still the distinguishing factor of humanity.

our decisions.³ Philosophers have almost unanimously argued that reason is a better guide to action than emotion. When I teach ethics, I illustrate this point by having college students imagine trying to study in their dorm room while their roommate is playing loud music. One's inclination (to use a Kantian term) is to do something like yell, hit the roommate, break the stereo, etc., all of which would probably not be the correct thing to do. We decide what we will do by reasoning; considering our different options and evaluating them according to some principle.

Is there ever a situation in which reason is not the best guide to action? This is a difficult question. The philosopher Pascal famously said, "The heart has its reasons, which reason does not know [at all]."⁴ This statement is often interpreted as being directed at romantic love, but Pascal clearly had faith in a god in mind. Romantic love is the category most often cited as one in which reason should play less of a role. This claim, however, is problematic. While it would be strange for a person to try to analyze a romantic relationship on a purely rational level, it is equally true that many people get into bad romantic relationships because of too little rational analysis of the character and compatibility of the person with whom they are involved.

Even taking the possible exceptions of religious faith (which will be discussed in detail later) and romance, it still seems likely that, for the most part, in most situations, the more we use reason to make decisions, the better off we will be. This has been the message of philosophers throughout history.

The Meaning of "Reasonable"

We can take it as good advice that we should be "reasonable." And we can take "reasonable" to mean "using our reason as much as we can and making our decisions based on the best application

---

3. Aristotle expands the list to seven: "all the actions of men must necessarily be referred to seven causes: chance, nature, compulsion, habit, reason, anger, and desire." *Rhetoric*, Book 1, Chapter 10.

4. Pascal, *Pensées*, #277.

The *Concept* of a Reasonable Christian Faith

of our reason to the situation or decision at hand." However, it is less clear what the opposite term, "unreasonable" means. Here is where one of the major problems related to faith and reason arises. One possible definition of "unreasonable" is "not arrived at through the use of reason." Another is "contradicting reason." If we accept the claim "Everyone should be reasonable," then we must accept the converse, "No one should be unreasonable." But since "unreasonable" is ambiguous, so is the claim that no one should be unreasonable. It could mean (a) "No one should accept anything as true that contradicts reason," or it could mean (b) "No one should accept anything as true that was not arrived at through the use of reason." Accepting something as true that contradicts reason is clearly unreasonable. If someone said, "there are square circles," or "two plus two equals five," we would be correct to respond that they are being unreasonable. But it is not so clear, and is in fact almost certainly false, that we should never accept anything as true *other* than what has arrived at through the use of reason, especially if this means "our own reason." We all reasonably accept many things as true that we didn't arrive at by our own reason. For instance, it is reasonable to believe that the sun is 93 million miles from the earth, although almost no one has evaluated that statement with their own reason. It is also reasonable to believe that there is a country called Japan even if one has never been there. A more difficult question is whether we should accept anything as true that was not arrived at by any human's reason. This is precisely where the discussion of faith and reason arises.

The New Atheists make clear that they hold science to be the ultimate authority by which to judge what is reasonable and what is unreasonable. This interpretation, I will argue, is flawed.

Science and Reason

What is the relationship between science and reason? "Science" is itself notoriously difficult to define. As a preliminary definition, we can take the OED definition: "the intellectual and practical activity encompassing the systematic study of the structure and behavior of the physical and natural world through observation and experiment."⁵ I will reword this definition into the terms of our discussion: "the use of reason to find explanations for events in the natural/physical world." The expression "observation and experiment" is a reference what scientists apply their reason to. We know about the natural world by observing it with our senses, and scientists do experiments by which they predict what observations a person would make if he or she were in a specific place under specific conditions (this is true even of microscopic or astronomic science—the instruments used tell us what we would experience if we could perceive the phenomena in question with our own senses).

The claim of the New Atheists amounts to "any ideas not arrived at through the scientific method is unreasonable." But is this true or reasonable? This question leads us into one of the oldest topics of philosophy, epistemology. Epistemology is the branch of philosophy that studies knowledge. It includes questions like "what can we know for sure?", "what are the sources of knowledge?", and "are there limits to knowledge?" The New Atheist claim is an epistemological claim; it is about what (valid) sources of knowledge there are. There have been two main epistemological positions through history. One is *empiricism*; it is the belief that all knowledge is arrived at by way of the 5 senses (sight, hearing, taste, touch, and smell). The other is *rationalism*; it is the belief that some knowledge comes from sources other than the 5 senses.

Empiricism makes a very strong claim. It is universal; it refers to ALL knowledge. Universal claims are notoriously difficult to maintain or argue for. All that is needed is a single counterexample to disprove the claim. Even if 99.9999% of our knowledge is empirical, that is not enough to validate empiricism. So, people can believe that the vast majority of our knowledge comes through the 5 senses without being an empiricist (I, for one, am such a person). Rationalism, on the other hand, is simply the denial of empiricism, and makes a much weaker claim. It only claims that

---

5. http://oxforddictionaries.com/definition/american_english/science?region=us&q=science.

The *Concept* of a Reasonable Christian Faith

NOT ALL knowledge comes through the senses. All it would take is a single instance of knowledge coming by a means other than the senses to validate rationalism. To be fair, it is difficult to cite a clear case of non-empirical knowledge. However, this is insufficient to disprove rationalism. We might discover clear cases of non-empirical knowledge tomorrow.

While rationalism is easy (theoretically) to prove (a single instance of non-empirical knowledge is all that is needed), I think empiricism is theoretically impossible to prove. There are two reasons for this. First, we could ask the empiricist, "how do you know that ALL knowledge comes through the 5 senses? Did you arrive at that knowledge empirically?" The answer must be "no"—what set of observations could establish the truth of that claim? It is impossible for empiricists to validate their own theory. That means that if we accept their claim, it leads us to reject the claim! In philosophy, this situation is called *self-referential incoherence*. The second reason is that, even if empiricists could show that all knowledge up until this point has been arrived at empirically, that could not prove that there is not another source of knowledge that we might find tomorrow that is non-empirical, which would disprove empiricism.

To return to our main topic, there is a very close connection between science and empiricism. Science is the study of the world through the 5 senses. The New Atheists, in their espousal of science, espouse empiricism. So, the weaknesses of empiricism as a philosophical position carry over to science. If the claim is "ALL valid knowledge must come through science," then, given our definition of science, it amounts to the claim that ALL valid knowledge must be arrived at through observation and experiment, which is by means of the 5 senses, which is empiricism. The same challenges apply.

The claim "All knowledge/ideas must come through science/empiricism" is both unverifiable and self-referentially incoherent. That doesn't mean that science is wrong or bad. It just means that, while science and empiricism can tell us a lot about the physical world (like how to cure diseases, how to fly airplanes, how to split atoms, etc.), there are questions that science cannot even address. Ironically, "is science the only way to acquire knowledge?" is one of the questions that science can't answer! To move from the claim that something has not been experienced to the claim that something *can* or *cannot* happen is to enter the realm of what I will henceforth call *scientism* (the unwarranted belief that science is the only valid source of human knowledge). The noun for a person who ascribes to scientism is difficult. It can't be "scientist," because that fails to distinguish between a reasonable acceptance of the methods of science (which I have) and an unreasonable dependence on the methods of science (which I do not have).[6] I will use "scientistic people" to refer to people who advocate scientism.

A common challenge to religion by scientistic people regards the possibility of miracles. Scientistic people argue that miracles cannot happen. However, the claim "miracles can't happen" is not a scientific claim and could never be validated by the scientific method (we will take "miracle" to mean "a suspension of the regular laws of nature by a supernatural being for a specific purpose"). Science is the study of human observations and the prediction of what one would observe in certain other situations. Science is the study of human experience, and, more, the study of regularities in human experience.[7] To take several of the central miracles related to Christianity, scientists can say "we (modern scientists) have never experienced a baby that was not conceived through the joining of a human egg and a human sperm" or "we (modern scientists) have never experienced water that instantaneously turned into wine" or "we (modern scientists) have never experienced someone rising from the dead," and these statements might all be

---

6. It is worth noting that a number of the world's best scientists assert that, while quantum physics is the best confirmed scientific theory in history, no one understands it. For instance, Richard Feynman, "I think I can safely say that nobody understands quantum mechanics." (https://www.bbvaopenmind.com/en/science/leading-figures/richard-feynman-the-physicist-who-didnt-understand-his-own-theories/). This seems to be, in itself, a strong argument against scientism, especially the "science has it all figured out" version.

7. This interpretation of science is well-attested in the early modern philosophers, Locke, Berkeley, Hume, and Kant.

The *Concept* of a Reasonable Christian Faith

true. But to go from those statements to the statements "no baby could be conceived without the joining of human egg and a human sperm" or "no instance of water turning instantaneously into wine could ever take place" or "no person could ever rise from the dead" is to draw unwarranted conclusions. Science, again, can tell us what normally happens or what can be predicted to happen, but science can never declare what *can* or *can't* happen in the world. Is it *reasonable* to believe that miracles can happen? That, again, depends on how you define "reasonable." There is nothing logically contradictory or impossible about the idea that there is a being beyond the natural world that could, if it wanted to, change the laws of nature in certain specific situations for particular reasons.[8] Therefore, although they may be very uncommon and few people may have experienced miracles, they are not *unreasonable* in the sense of "going against reason." To claim that belief in miracles is unreasonable is to misunderstand the definition of "reasonable." In fact, the person who rejects the possibility of miracles is more unreasonable than the one who accepts their possibility. It would unreasonable (because no sufficient argument can be made for it) to reject the possible existence of anything that is logically possible.

Reason and Consistency

One rational principle that I will use in this book is the idea of *consistency*. Logically, if two (or more) statements are *consistent*, it is possible for them to be true at the same time. The statements "it is 10:00 a.m. in Los Angeles" and "it is 1:00 p.m. in New York" are consistent; they can both be true at the same time. If two (or more) statements are *inconsistent*, then they cannot be true at the same time. The statements "the sun is 93 million miles from the earth" and "the sun is 10 miles from the earth" are inconsistent; if either one of them is true, the other is necessarily false. In the case of

---

8. The question of why a supernatural being would want to intervene in the world and why it would intervene in some cases and not others, are important and difficult questions, but are not relevant to the current discussion. I am only talking about possibilities here.

inconsistent statements, it is possible for them all to be false ("the sun is 10 miles from the earth" and "the sun is 100 miles from the earth" are inconsistent and both false); it is just not possible for them all to be true. I will be making use of the principle that it is irrational to assert that both of a pair of inconsistent statements are true.

Rational/Philosophical Arguments for God

Plato

One of the most influential writings in Western history is Plato's *Allegory of the Cave*. Plato was a Greek philosopher who lived from 428 – 348 B.C. While it is a long reading, it is so influential and so well expressed that it is worth reading in its entirety. Socrates is having a conversation with a friend, Glaucon:

> **Socrates:** And now, let me show in a figure how far our nature is enlightened or unenlightened: Imagine that human beings live in a cave; they have been here since their childhood, and have their legs and necks chained so that they cannot move, and can only see ahead of them, since the chains keep them from turning their heads. Above and behind them a fire is blazing, and between the fire and the prisoners there is a low wall, like the screen which shadow-puppet performers have in front of them, over which they show the puppets.
> **Glaucon:** I see.
> **Socrates:** And do you see, men passing along the wall carrying all sorts of vessels, and statues and figures of animals made of wood and stone and various materials, which appear over the wall? Some of them are talking, others silent.
> **Glaucon: You have shown me a strange image and they are strange prisoners.**
> **Socrates:** Like ourselves, I replied; and they see only their own shadows, or the shadows of one another, which the fire throws on the opposite wall of the cave?

Glaucon: True; how could they see anything but the shadows if they were never allowed to move their heads?

Socrates: And of the objects which are being carried in like manner they would only see the shadows?

Glaucon: Yes.

Socrates: And if they were able to converse with one another, would they not suppose that they were naming what was actually before them?

Glaucon: Very true.

Socrates: And suppose further that the prison had an echo which came from the other side, would they not be sure to fancy when one of the passers-by spoke that the voice which they heard came from the passing shadow?

Glaucon: No question.

Socrates: To them, the truth would be literally nothing but the shadows of the images.

Glaucon: That is certain.

Socrates: And now look again, and see what will happen if the prisoners are released. At first, if one of them is set free and made to stand up and turn around look towards the fire, he will feel sharp pains; the glare will distress him, and he will be unable to see the realities that were casting the shadows. Now imagine that someone explains to him that what he saw before was an illusion, but that now, when he is approaching nearer to being and his eye is turned towards more real existence, he has a clearer vision. What will be his reply? And you may further imagine that his instructor is pointing to the objects as they pass and requiring him to name them—wouldn't he be perplexed? Wouldn't he think that the shadows which he formerly saw are truer than the objects which are now shown to him?

Glaucon: Far truer.

Socrates: And if he is compelled to look straight at the fire, wouldn't he have a pain in his eyes which would make him turn away to look back at the shadows that he can see? And wouldn't the shadows seem clearer than the things which are now being shown to him?

Glaucon: True.

Socrates: And suppose once more, that he is reluctantly dragged up a steep and rugged ascent, and held fast until he's forced into the presence of the sun himself, is he not likely to be pained and irritated? When he approaches the sun his eyes will be dazzled, and he will not be able to see anything at all of what are we think are realities.

Glaucon: Not all in a moment.

Socrates: He will need to grow accustomed to the sight of the upper world. And first he will see the shadows best, next the reflections of men and other objects in the water, and then the objects themselves; then he will gaze upon the light of the moon and the stars and the spangled heaven; and he will see the sky and the stars by night better than the sun or the light of the sun by day?

Glaucon: Certainly.

Socrates: Last of he will be able to see the sun, and not mere reflections of him in the water, but he will see him in his own proper place, and not in another; and he will contemplate him as he is.

Glaucon: Certainly.

Socrates: He will then proceed to argue that this is he who gives the season and the years, and is the guardian of all that is in the visible world, and in a certain way the cause of all things which he and his fellows have been accustomed to behold?

Glaucon: Clearly, he would first see the sun and then reason about him.

Socrates: And when he remembered his old habitation, and the wisdom of the den and his fellow-prisoners, do you not suppose that he would be happy about the change, and pity them?

Glaucon: Certainly, he would.

Socrates: And if they were in the habit of conferring honors among themselves on those who were quickest to observe the passing shadows and to remark which of them went before, and which followed after, and which were together; and who were therefore best able to draw conclusions as to the future, do you think that he would care for such honors and glories, or envy the possessors of them? (. . .)

The *Concept* of a Reasonable Christian Faith

Glaucon: Yes, I think that he would rather experience anything than believe these false notions and live in this miserable manner.

Socrates: Imagine once more, that he . . . is put back in his old situation; would he not be certain to have his eyes full of darkness?

Glaucon: To be sure.

Socrates: And if there were a contest, and he had to compete in measuring the shadows with the prisoners who had never moved out of the den, while his sight was still weak, and before his eyes had become steady (and the time which would be needed to acquire this new habit of sight might be very considerable) would he not be ridiculous? Men would say of him that up he went and down he came without his eyes; and that it was better not even to think of ascending; and if any one tried to loose another and lead him up to the light, let them only catch the offender, and they would put him to death.

Glaucon: No question.

Socrates: This entire allegory, you may now append, dear Glaucon, to the previous argument; the prison-house is the world of sight, the light of the fire is the sun, and you will not misapprehend me if you interpret the journey upwards to be the ascent of the soul into the intellectual world according to my poor belief, which, at your desire, I have expressed whether rightly or wrongly god knows. But, whether true or false, my opinion is that in the world of knowledge the idea of good appears last of all, and is seen only with an effort; and, when seen, is also inferred to be the universal author of all things beautiful and right, parent of light and of the lord of light in this visible world, and the immediate source of reason and truth in the intellectual; and that this is the power upon which he who would act rationally, either in public or private life must have his eye fixed.[9]

The depth and complexity of Plato's vision here is remarkable (remember, Plato wrote this around 400 years before Christ). Our physical universe is represented by the cave (notice that the fire

---

9. Plato, *The Republic*, Book VII.

inside the cave represents our sun). But this world, in the allegory, is a world of shadows and "illusion." Everything in the cave is a "copy" or "imitation" of something outside the cave. Ultimately, in the world outside the cave there is a sun, which is responsible for the existence of everything, and is the most "real" thing. This is what Plato says about the being that the sun represents (he calls it the "idea of good"): "[it is] the universal author of all things beautiful and right, parent of light and of the lord of light in this visible world [our sun], and the immediate source of reason and truth in the intellectual [world]; and that this is the power upon which he who would act rationally, either in public or private life must have his eye fixed." This is as clear and beautiful a description of a single god who created everything as can be found. Notice the connection between morality (goodness) and reason in this being—the same being is responsible for both.

The main point that I want to stress in this text is the argument behind Plato's position. For Plato, our universe, the world of experience, is shadowy and less than real. This world is not "real" enough to account for its own existence. It can't explain itself. Plato posited another world "beyond" or "besides" this one that is more real, and ultimately a being that is so "real" that it can be responsible for both its own existence and the existence of this world. For Plato (and Socrates), the existence of this world *requires* the existence of such a being. That is, they would argue that if one is rational, one is required by reason to believe in the existence of this world and being.[10]

Aristotle

Aristotle (384 BC – 322 BC) was Plato's student, as Plato was Socrates' student. While Aristotle disagreed with Plato regarding many things, he presented a similar and similarly famous argument for the existence of a god. Here is what he wrote:

---

10. It is also noteworthy that Socrates and Plato were directly referencing some "Pre-Socratic" philosophers, primarily Parmenides.

The *Concept* of a Reasonable Christian Faith

> Since everything that is in motion must be moved by something, let us take the case in which a thing is in motion and is moved by something that is itself in motion, and that again is moved by something else that is in motion, and that by something else, and so on continually: then the series cannot go on to infinity, but there must be some first mover. For let us suppose that this is not so and take the series to be infinite. The things moved and the movers must be continuous or in contact with one another, so that together they all form a single unity: in any case since the things in motion are infinite in number the whole motion will be infinite, if, as is theoretically possible, each motion is either equal to or greater than that which follows it in the series: for we shall take as actual that which is theoretically possible. If, then, A, B, G, D form an infinite magnitude that passes through the motion EZHO in the finite time K, this involves the conclusion that an infinite motion is passed through in a finite time: and whether the magnitude in question is finite or infinite this is in either case impossible. Therefore the series must come to an end, and there must be a first mover and a first moved.[11]

Things move, argues Aristotle. Things that move are generally moved by something else. The thing that moved the last thing was itself moved by something before it. So, we can imagine a series of things moving other things going back in time. For instance, imagine you are standing beside a train track. A train is going by. The train is very long, so you cannot see where it begins or ends. Each car in the train represents one of the "things" Aristotle is referring to. The argument is this: how many train cars can there be between you and the engine on the train? There can be very, very many. But there is one number of train cars that it cannot be. There cannot be an infinite number of train cars between you and the engine. Why not? This is the tricky, but essential part of the argument. The train is moving past the spot at which you stand. That means that the entire train (so far) must have moved past that spot. If the entire

---

11. Aristotle, *Physics*, Book 7. I have edited and updated the text for readability.

train has moved past that spot, then it must have done so in a finite amount of time. But if there were an infinite number of train cars between you and the engine, then the train could not have moved past you in a finite amount of time. So, the case of an infinitely long train is impossible (which is another way of saying it goes against reason). The conclusion is, the train must be finitely long.

Aristotle has in mind the physical processes of the world. He is actually working like a scientist here. The "movements" he's talking about are physical processes causing (or moving or changing) other physical processes. He imagines a series of physical processes going back in time, each being caused by a previous physical process (the train). How far back can this series of physical processes go? It can go back a very long way. But there is one length of time it cannot go back—it cannot go back infinitely far. Why not? The answer is like the one in the train analogy. We are observing the series of physical processes in finite time. If the series of physical processes (going back) was infinitely long, then it could not be a part of any finite time sequence of which we are a part. But the physical processes are part of the time sequence of which we are a part. So, the series cannot be infinitely long. The conclusion, then (see the last line of the quotation) is that there must be a "first mover." That means that, for Aristotle, like for Plato and Socrates, the physical world that we see must have another type of being that is "beyond" it and that started it. If there is no first mover, there is no physical world. Aristotle goes on in another place to describe what he thinks the first mover must be like:

> The heavens and the world of nature depend on such a First Principle, then. And it is a life such as the best which we enjoy, since its actuality is also pleasure. And thinking in itself deals with that which is best in itself, and that which is thinking in the fullest sense with that which is best in the fullest sense. And thought thinks on itself because it shares the nature of the object of thought; for it becomes an object of thought in coming into contact with and thinking its objects, so that thought and object of thought are the same. The possession rather than the receptivity is the divine element which thought

The *Concept* of a Reasonable Christian Faith

seems to contain, and the act of contemplation is what is most pleasant and best. If, then, god is always in that good state in which we sometimes are, this compels our wonder; and if [god is] in a better [state] this compels it yet more. And god is in a better state. And life also belongs to god; for the actuality of thought is life, and god is that actuality; and god's self-dependent actuality is life most good and eternal. We say therefore that god is a living being, eternal, most good, so that life and duration continuous and eternal belong to god; for this is god.[12]

Plato's and Aristotle's arguments are *rational* arguments. In this case, "rational" is being opposed to "theological." These arguments are rational because they do not appeal to any religious texts or authorities or traditions. They appeal only to human reason. But they are also rational as opposed to empirical. When he started with observations of things in the world, the empirical evidence suggested to Aristotle that there must be a "being" beyond the physical world. The existence of the physical world itself suggests this to Aristotle, like Plato, because he believes that the physical processes of the world cannot explain themselves; they require a deeper explanation, one that goes beyond the world. This kind of argument was developed by a number of Christian, Jewish, and Muslim philosophers over the 1500 years following Aristotle. I will now turn to the most famous of these, by Saint Thomas Aquinas.

St. Thomas Aquinas

St. Thomas Aquinas (1225–1274) was a Catholic theologian and philosopher. He was heavily influenced by Aristotle; his work was an effort to synthesize the philosophical ideas of Aristotle with theological ideas from Christianity. The arguments discussed here are part of a series of arguments known as the "five ways," which is short for "five ways of proving god's existence using only rational arguments." They are developments of the argument we just

---

12. Aristotle, *Metaphysics*, Book 12, Part 6. I have edited and updated the text for readability.

considered from Aristotle. The structure and conclusions are very similar. The first is really a reproduction of Aristotle's argument from motion. I will discuss only two of the "ways." It is important to note that, while Aquinas was a Christian theologian, these are *rational* arguments, in the sense that they do not appeal to any Christian or biblical ideas for the arguments themselves:

> The second way is from the nature of cause-and-effect. In the world of sense we find things causing effects. There is no case known (neither is it, indeed, possible) in which a thing causes itself; for so it would exist before it existed, which is impossible. Now a chain of causes cannot go on to infinity, because to take away the cause is to take away the effect. Therefore, if there be no first cause among causes, there will be no ultimate, nor any intermediate cause. But if the chain of causes went on to infinity, there would be no first cause, so there wouldn't be any later effects, nor any intermediate causes; all of which is plainly false. Therefore it is necessary to admit a first cause, to which everyone gives the name of God.[13]

This argument is very similar to Aristotle's argument from motion. Aquinas changes "movement" and "mover" to "cause." Aquinas notes the series of causes and effects we see in the world. Like Aristotle, he focuses on the point that the series cannot be infinitely long, but uses a slightly different argument. His argument is that if the series was infinitely long, there would be no "first cause." But without a first cause (to start the series), there would be no effects; no series. But there is a series—we see it! The conclusion is that there must be a (first, initiating) cause of the (physical) series of causes and effects that we experience.

While Aquinas doesn't develop them here, we can draw some further rational conclusions from this argument. The first is that the first cause cannot itself be caused by something else. The reason for this is simple; if something else caused the first cause, then this would not be the first cause, the other cause would! So, logically, the first cause must be *uncaused*. This is a very deep and

---

13. Aquinas, *Summa Theologica*, Part 1, Question 2, Article 3.

The *Concept* of a Reasonable Christian Faith

important philosophical concept. Many people ask the question, "If God made the world, then who made God?" The answer is, "*No one* made God." To be uncaused *is to never have come into existence*, which in turn means to have *always* existed. The argument is that to have a world that came into existence (or a world in which things come into existence) *requires* that there be a being that has always existed. Without that being, there is no *reasonable* explanation for this world.[14] Thus, Aquinas, following Aristotle, concludes, based on his reason, that there must be such a being (which he takes to be the Christian God, but which I am not claiming at this point).

The next argument is very difficult, but worth looking at:

> The third way is taken from possibility and necessity. We see things that are possible to be and not to be, since they are found to come into existence, and to go out of existence, and consequently, they are possible to be and not to be. But it is impossible for these to exist always, because if it is possible for something not to exist, then at some time it doesn't exist. So, if everything is possible not to be, then at one time there could have been nothing in existence. Now if this were true, even now there would be nothing in existence, because nothing comes from nothing! Therefore, if at one time nothing was in existence, it would have been impossible for anything to have begun to exist; and thus even now nothing would be in existence--which is absurd. Therefore, not all beings are merely possible, but there must exist something

---

14. Richard Dawkins makes this mistake in *The Blind Watchmaker*: "To explain the origin of the DNA/protein machine by invoking a supernatural Designer is to explain precisely nothing, for it leaves unexplained the origin of the Designer. You have to say something like 'God was always there', and if you allow yourself that kind of lazy way out, you might as well just say 'DNA was always there', or 'Life was always there', and be done with it." Aristotle's and Aquinas' point is that the uncaused cause *does* explain something. It is required for there to be *any* explanation of the physical world. It is true that the question of why there is an uncaused cause has no answer. But it is not true that the claim "the physical world has always existed" is as reasonable as "an uncaused cause has always existed and must exist if a physical world exists." Richard Dawkins, *The Blind Watchmaker*, 141.

that exists necessarily. Therefore we must postulate the existence of some being having of itself its own necessity. This all men speak of as God.[15]

To explain this argument, I begin by introducing some philosophical terms. Aquinas uses the term "necessary". A *necessary* being is a being that cannot *not* exist. In other words, it is *impossible* for a necessary being *not* to exist (This definition includes a double negative, which makes it difficult). The other kind of beings Aquinas refers to are "things that are possible to be and not to be." He mentions that we see things coming into existence and going out of existence. For instance, the computer I am typing on came into existence and will go out of existence. The house I live in, the car I drive, the United States, all came into existence and will go out of existence. The philosophical term for such beings is *contingent* beings. A *contingent* being is one that does *not necessarily* exist, or one for whom it is possible for it to either exist or not exist.

Aquinas begins with the point that there are contingent beings. This point is rationally irrefutable. We are surrounded by contingent beings. Now, in a move that traces back to Aristotle, Aquinas argues that the very existence of contingent beings *rationally requires* that there be at least one necessary being. The argument is complex, but goes like this. If everything were a contingent being (which comes into and goes out of existence), then at some point in the past, it is possible that nothing at all existed. In other words, if it is possible for each contingent being not to exist, then it could be that they all *didn't* exist at some point, in which case nothing would exist. But if there were a time in the past when nothing existed, then nothing would ever have begun to exist, because nothing can come from nothing!

What follows from the argument so far is that there cannot ever have been in the past a time when nothing existed.[16] This is in itself quite a profound and remarkable conclusion. But Aquinas goes further. If everything were a contingent being, then, if there

---

15. Aquinas, *Summa Theologia*, Part 1, Question 2, Article 3. I have edited and updated the text for readability

16. See also Locke, *An Essay Concerning Human Understanding*, 835.

The *Concept* of a Reasonable Christian Faith

were only contingent beings, then there would have had to be a time in the past when nothing existed. Aquinas does not explain this step too clearly, but I think he has this in mind: it seems to be a property of contingent things that they are caused to exist by other things. It seems difficult to imagine anything in our physical world that wasn't caused to exist by something else. The only other options are that nothing caused the thing, which is impossible, or that the thing caused itself, which is impossible, or that the thing has always existed, which doesn't seem to be the case with anything in our physical world, including the physical world itself.[17] Now if the contingent things that we see are all caused by other things, there must be a series of contingent things (causing other contingent things) going back in time. The question is, how far can this series go (this question should sound familiar!)? As in the earlier arguments, the answer is, it can go very far, but it cannot go back in time infinitely. This means that there must be a first contingent being. But then we have to ask, where did this first contingent being come from? The possibilities, again, are (a) that it was caused by another contingent being, (b) that it was caused by nothing, (c) that it caused itself, or (d) that it was caused by a necessary being. The answer cannot be (a), because this is the *first* contingent being. The answer cannot be (b), because nothing can come from nothing. Answer (c) is impossible; nothing can cause itself. So we are left with only one possible cause of the first contingent being: a necessary being. Thus, Aquinas argues, the existence of contingent beings, which is undoubtable, requires the existence of a necessary being. The argument for and the qualities of this Necessary Being connect with the argument for and qualities of the First Cause and the argument for and the qualities of Aristotle's First Mover. It has always existed and it preceded and caused the contingent, physical world in which we live.

---

17. Someone might point out that Aristotle believed that the physical world has always existed, which is true. But he still believed that the physical world must be *caused* by the First Mover; as long as the First Mover exists, the physical world exists, but without the First Mover, the physical world would not exist.

A Reasonable Christian Faith

Averroes and William Paley

There is one more influential classical philosophical argument for the existence of a god. This one is both better known and more controversial. It is generally referred to as the Design Argument. It is best known in the form presented by William Paley regarding a watch, but an earlier version is found in the work of the Muslim philosopher, Averroes, in the 12th century A.D.:

> When a man sees a thing made in a certain shape, proportion and fashion, and a particular advantage is derived from it, for a purpose which is to be attained, so that it becomes clear to him, that if it had not been found in that shape, and proportion, then that advantage would have been lacking in it, he comes to know for certain that there is a maker of that thing, and that he made it in that shape and proportion, for a set purpose. For it is not possible that all those qualities serving that purpose could be found in that thing by chance alone. For instance, if a man sees a stone on the ground in a shape fit for sitting, and finds its proportions and fashion of the same kind, then he would come to know that it was made by a maker, and that he made it and placed it there. But when he sees nothing in it which may have made it fit for sitting then he becomes certain that its existence in the place was by chance only, without its being fashioned by any maker.[18]

Averroes' point relates to what we take to be a reasonable explanation for something. He uses the analogy of a stone "in a shape for sitting," which, unfortunately, is not very clear.

Here is Paley's argument, written about 600 years later:

> In crossing a heath, suppose I pitched my foot against a stone, and were asked how the stone came to be there; I might possibly answer, that, for any thing I knew to the contrary, it had lain there forever: nor would it perhaps be very easy to show the absurdity of this answer. But suppose I had found a watch upon the ground, and it should be inquired how the watch happened to be in that

---

18. Averroes, *The Philosophy and Theology of Averroes*.

The *Concept* of a Reasonable Christian Faith

place; I should hardly think of the answer which I had before given, that, for any thing I knew, the watch might have always been there. Yet why should not this answer serve for the watch as well as for the stone? Why is it not as admissible in the second case, as in the first? For this reason, and for no other, viz. that, when we come to inspect the watch, we perceive (what we could not discover in the stone) that its several parts are framed and put together for a purpose, e.g. that they are so formed and adjusted as to produce motion, and that motion so regulated as to point out the hour of the day; that, if the different parts had been differently shaped from what they are, of a different size from what they are, or placed after any other manner, or in any other order, than that in which they are placed, either no motion at all would have been carried on in the machine, or none which would have answered the use that is now served by it.[19]

The question here, again, is, "what counts as a reasonable explanation of something?" The answer, from both Averroes and Paley, is partly that it depends on what you are explaining. If you see a rock sitting on the road and you ask, "where did this rock come from?" (not just, "how did this rock happen to get onto this road?" but "how did this rock come into existence to begin with?"), it would be a reasonable explanation to say "it was formed millions of years ago by some geological processes and was pushed to the surface in an earthquake and broke off the cliff up there and rolled down here to the road." This explanation appeals only to natural (physical) processes. It is sufficient (i.e., enough) to explain the existence and location of the rock. But now, suppose you found a watch on the road. Would it be a reasonable explanation of the watch to say "the atoms formed over millions of years into the different pieces of metal and plastic and glass, and the wind and rain moved the pieces around over a long period of time and this watch was formed right here"? Almost everyone would say "no." The question is, why? The reason, for both Averroes and Paley, is that there is something about the structure of the watch that requires

---

19. Paley and Holley, *Natural Theology*, 1.

additional explanation; the natural explanation is not sufficient. The additional feature of the watch is *purpose*. The parts of the watch have particular shapes and a particular arrangement so that they all seem to be working together toward an end or a goal. The key question, then, is, why does a structure that leads us to think something has a purpose make us believe that a natural explanation is not sufficient? The answer, I think, is experience. In our dealings with the world we notice that things we find in nature, like rocks and lakes and mountains (I leave plants and animals aside for the moment) tend to be organized randomly, without any structure that seems to imply purpose. Things that contain specific, special arrangements that seem to imply purpose are things like watches, airplanes, houses, or beaver dams. We notice that these things are all made by humans or animals. What is the difference between humans and animals on the one hand, and rocks and dirt on the other? Humans and animals are alive and have goals and purposes, while rocks and mountains aren't and don't. So we form, as a general hypothesis about the world, the claim that things that have specially organized structures that seem to work together for a purpose tend to be constructed by beings (people and animals) that construct the things for the purpose. Then we test and revise this hypothesis against our experience. The correlation is in fact, very strong; virtually everything we see around us that has specially organized structures working together for a purpose was made by a living being that has purposes, and virtually nothing that was not made by a living being that has purposes (rocks, lakes, mountains) seems to have specially ordered structures working together for a purpose. So we develop an empirical law: *things exhibit specially organized structures that work together for a purpose only if they are constructed by a living being that has goals and purposes.*[20]

The point of setting up this principle is to use it to evaluate something. Averroes and Paley have something very specific in mind: the universe. They think that the universe exhibits the kind of specially organized structures that work together for a purpose.

---

20. The word "empirical", again, means "based on observation and experience."

The *Concept* of a Reasonable Christian Faith

However, I'm not sure that the universe as a whole does exhibit this structure, so I'm going to change the analogy somewhat. I will take "life" or "living thing" as the object in question. Living things (mice, humans, insects) exhibit very complexly organized and inter-related structures that clearly work together for a purpose: survival. So, by our principle, which seems quite reasonable, based on our experience of the world, it is reasonable to conclude that living things must be (or have been) constructed by a living being with goals and purposes. Since our principle is reasonable, based on our experience, our conclusion must be called reasonable. I am not claiming to have *proven* anything, because, as we have seen, inductive (experience-based) arguments can never prove anything; but they can make some conclusions more probable than others.

Now, most contemporary evolutionary scientists will say that this conclusion is false; that it is possible to explain life appealing only to natural processes. (Let me be clear at the outset that I am not questioning evolution as an empirical theory based on descent-with-genetic-modifications and adaptation to the environment. I am discussing the reasonableness of explanations for the existence of living things in our world). To claim that a belief is false is not the same as to claim that it is unreasonable. Reasonableness has to do with how one comes to believe a claim, or with continuing to believe a claim in the face of evidence that goes against it. I have already shown that in the first sense, it is quite reasonable to believe that living thing were constructed by a living being with goals and purposes. The question now becomes, "has contemporary evolutionary science provided compelling evidence that life was not constructed by a living being with goals and purposes?" I would argue that it has not. Evolutionary science tells us a lot about patterns of descent-with-modification, and it identifies a vehicle of change over time; genetic modification and environmental pressure. And evolutionary scientists propose that life may have arisen here by natural processes. The question is, which is more reasonable to believe; that life arose through random natural processes, or that life was constructed by a living being with goals and purposes? I claim that is at least is reasonable to believe that life was constructed by a being with goals and purposes, based on the evidence of a very consistent experience of the world, is the latter.

Conclusion

The argument so far has aimed to establish a limited conclusion: that there is a rational (i.e., available to reason) basis to believe that the (physical, changing, contingent) world that we experience requires, as a sufficient explanation for its existence, a being that is unchanging and necessary (and non-physical, although I have not discussed that aspect of this being).

Two notes about these arguments. First, other than the teleological argument, they are not scientific or empirical arguments. However, they would argue that the nature of the being they are describing precludes the possibility of knowing it empirically—they would argue that the existence of this being is rationally necessary. So, to them, the charge that science can't identify or observe this being is pointless (and in fact it is actually required by the argument).

Second, scientist people might argue that science has dispelled the need for such a being (this is precisely what Nietzsche's infamous phrase "God is dead" refers to), and that these philosophers simply had not experienced modern science. I believe that this response also misses the point. First, to make such a statement is to go beyond the bounds of science, into metaphysics. What empirical experiment or observation could validate the claim "science explains (or can eventually explain) everything"? This is not a scientific claim in any sense. Science has explained and can explain a lot, but to make claims about what science can or will explain is not a scientific claim. Second, I believe that none of these ancient philosophers would change their argument at all after encountering modern science. Aristotle was really the first empirical scientist; he wrote volumes about how the physical world was structured and arranged. His point was specifically that no physical explanation could serve as an explanation for the existence of the physical world itself.

The *Concept* of a Reasonable Christian Faith

As a final point, some modern scientifically-minded people claim that they don't care what the ultimate explanation of the physical world is. This is a possible position, but this is not a position that was arrived at *rationally*. This is simply a decision that one might make to stop the investigation. Surely this argument is not valid: because I don't care what's beyond the physical world, there must not be anything beyond the physical world! Another related argument is self-contradictory: I don't care what's beyond the physical world, therefore I don't believe there is anything beyond the physical world. To form a belief is to care! Someone who holds this position must, rationally, refrain from engaging in the discussion at all.

The point, for now, is that there are arguments that appeal to human reason, crafted by very intelligent, very rational people, that conclude that there is a being beyond this world that must have brought this world into existence. For someone who finds these arguments convincing, they provide a reasonable basis for believing that such a being exists. Of course, these arguments don't say much about what such a being is like and the being they describe is not necessarily the god of Christianity, on whom I will focus later.

But there are some attributes we can glean from these arguments. In Aristotle's description, there are references to a single being (Aristotle uses the singular, "god"), life (related to the best life that humans can have), pleasure, thinking and contemplation (related to, but going beyond the best thinking of humans), "goodness" (related to, but better than "that good state in we sometimes are"), "Self-dependent actuality," and finally, in conclusion, "We say therefore that god is a living being, eternal, most good, so that life and duration continuous and eternal belong to god." These are cryptic descriptions, but they propose a series of attributes that Aristotle thinks this being must have. To these, Aquinas adds the attributes of being "uncaused" and "necessary" and Averroes and Paley add intelligence and having goals and ends. Since the god in all of these cases creates the world, we can take it that this being is powerful (at least powerful enough to create the physical universe and life). The question of why the world is like it is will be addressed in a later section.

This is a not-insubstantial list of attributes posited by the philosophical argument for the existence of a being beyond this world. As a last point, I simply reiterate that none of these arguments are theological arguments—none of them require anything more than our reason to be supported. We can say, as a preliminary conclusion, that there is a reasonable basis to believe that there is a being such as has been described so far.

Some Limitations on What God Must Be Like

We have seen in the previous sections that there is a reasonable argument that there is a being, God,[21] that is powerful, intelligent, and that has goals or intentions. It is possible, given these characteristics, that God also has characteristics such as that God isn't aware of the universe or humans, or that God is aware of, but doesn't care one way or the other about humans, or even that God dislikes humans and enjoys torturing them.

However, I argue that if God has any of these characteristics, then we as humans must either not care about God or even dislike and resist God. Again, it is possible that God dislikes humans and gives them orders and intends to punish (by which I mean to harm) humans that don't follow God's orders. It is possible that many or even most humans will follow God's orders in order not to be harmed by God. But I believe that, given the kind of being that humans are, no human can follow God willingly in that case, and that no human can have any positive feelings for, much less, love or worship God if God is like that. I want to provide a philosophical argument for that belief.

---

21. So far, I've been talking about "god" in a general sense, and have been using "god" without a capital G. Henceforth, since I will be talking about a more specific concept of God, I will use "God" with a capital G.

The *Concept* of a Reasonable Christian Faith

Happiness

Aristotle, in his book *The Nichomachean Ethics*, begins his discussion by talking about what motivates humans to act.[22] In my ethics courses, I do an exercise to illustrate this point. Suppose we ask (or actually ask) someone, "why are you doing that?" It doesn't matter what they are doing; they may be painting a picture or digging a ditch or taking a class. In response, says Aristotle, people will begin by giving reasons like "I'm painting because I love to paint," or "I am digging a ditch because I want to make money" or "I am taking a class because I want an education." But then Aristotle suggests that you keep asking them "why do you want that?" And they will continue for a while to give reasons like "I want to make money because I want to have a nice house and for my family to have enough food to eat." But eventually, if you keep asking "but why do you want that?", everyone's answer will converge on one answer; "because I want to be happy." Aristotle then makes several interesting points about this exercise. First, all of the goals or reasons up until "I want to be happy" are *intermediate* goals; they are all done for the sake of another goal (go to work to make money to buy food and clothing, etc.). But when you ask people (as I ask my students) why they want to be happy, they can't answer the question. They say things like "I don't want to be unhappy" or "It's better than the alternative (unhappiness)", which are just different formulations of "I want to be happy." So Aristotle says that happiness is a *final* goal: it is done for its own sake, not for the sake of any other goal. And he says that happiness is the *only* final goal that humans have. The conclusion of this exercise is that the primary motivation for anything that humans do is the desire to be happy.

The second part of this idea is that happiness and reason are related closely to each other. Reason, again, is the capacity to make decisions based on the evaluation of evidence. Striving toward happiness is a matter of making decisions about what to do. Ultimately, then, reason is the tool that we use to try to reach our final end, happiness.

22. Aristotle, *Nichomachean Ethics*, Book 1, Part 7.

Let me forestall some potential misunderstandings of this idea. First, although it may sound like Aristotle is promoting egoism or selfishness, he is not. It may (and seems to) turn out that human happiness is essentially connected with being in positive relationships with other humans, so our own happiness is related to the happiness of the people around us. Second, not every path that is supposed to lead to happiness actually leads to happiness—many people find that what they thought would lead them to happiness doesn't in fact do so. Third, in some cases the drive toward happiness is thwarted, and people must choose what they perceive to be the action that gets them the closest to happiness, even if both actions leave the person far from actual happiness. I believe that cases in which people choose addictions or violence or egoism are usually cases in which they perceive that the path they have chosen is the best they can do given the circumstances they face. Fourth, the best way to achieve happiness is a very large mystery. People have been arguing about it throughout human history. The philosophers I have been discussing have all made the argument that, since we were created by God and we get reason from God, happiness will ultimately be related to somehow knowing or being connected with God.

These reflections influence my view of God. First, they don't guarantee that God is not an uncaring or punishing God. However, since we are taking it that we have been created by God, it would seem unreasonable that that kind of being would create humans with a primary motivational drive that God didn't care about or intended to thwart. Second, they support my belief that our belief or non-belief in God is also motivated primarily by our desire to be happy. It is possible that our belief in and commitment to God are based on fear of punishment (not being punished is better than being punished). But fear is far from happiness (it is essentially unhappiness), so to follow God in that way is to live a life in which our primary motivation for acting is thwarted. I believe that it is impossible for humans to have positive regard for, to worship, and especially to love, a being that they recognize (overtly or not) has the intention to thwart their primary motivation. In this case, I

The *Concept* of a Reasonable Christian Faith

agree with the atheists; if God is like that, then God is not worthy of our love or worship.[23]

Given this argument, I conclude that we have good reason to believe that God is a being that cares about human happiness and intends for humans to be happy. This seems to me also to argue that God is happy—when Aristotle talks about God experiencing pleasure, I think he means "happy" in the sense of what humans are striving for when they seek to be happy.

A REASONABLE *CHRISTIAN* FAITH

Taoism and Religion

It might seem strange to some people to begin a discussion of Christianity with a discussion of Taoism. But there is a reason for this. I will be talking a lot about *interpreting* certain claims and events. But interpretation requires a framework. I will use Taoism to argue for a certain framework for interpreting religious claims and events.

The *Tao Te Ching* is a notoriously abstract and difficult text. Any interpretation of it is tentative. But I think my interpretation is consistent with the message of the text. The first lines of the *Tao Te Ching* are:

> The Tao that can be told is not the eternal Tao.
> The name that can be named is not the eternal name.
> The nameless is the beginning of heaven and earth.
> The named is the mother of ten thousand things.[24]

To begin with a translational issue, the Chinese term "tao," simply means "way." We can take "Tao" here to refer to "the ultimate Way or the ultimate reality." The term "name" appears several times in the opening stanzas. I will take "name" to mean "word" or "term"—to name something is to apply a word or term to it

---

23. It is also possible that people choose not to believe in god because they think that (believing in) god will lead them away from happiness.

24. Tsu, *Tao Te Ching*, Chapter 1.

("noun" derives from the Latin "nomen", or "name"). Any time we encounter the idea of naming things, we will think of language. Language is the result of naming the things we encounter in the world around us. The second line of the first stanza makes a negative claim: no words or terms that we (humans) use can name the Tao. I take this to mean that whatever we describe with human language, we are not describing the ultimate reality. Connecting with the philosophical arguments from the first chapter, language refers to the changing and non-enduring world around us. But the Tao is beyond this world. It is responsible for the world that we experience and name, but it is not that world.

To develop my interpretation, I must delve into the concept of language. Imagine a group of people, thousands of years ago, that are just beginning to create and use language; they are creating names, words, for the things around them. The environment around them will affect the words they create. If there are lions that might eat them, they will have to create words like "Lion" and "Run!" If they have to hunt gazelles for food, they will have to create words like "Gazelle" and "Spear." The words and language that they need to survive in the world will be affected by the environment they live in and the life they live. On the other hand, if a group of people, when forming a language, lived in an agricultural environment with no predatory animals, the words they would need would be different. They would need words like "season" and "crop" and "plant" and "harvest." The point is that two different groups of people, in different circumstances, would create different languages (there would clearly be some overlap, as we see in different languages, but lots of differences). The different languages they create, because they are based on different experiences of the world, would be, in a sense, different views of the world. The *Tao Te Ching* seems to me to be addressing this aspect of language.

The second line of the second stanza says, "having a name, it [the Tao] is the mother of all things." I take that to mean that to think about or talk about "things", humans have to apply names to the objects. Naming something (i.e., "dog") is to give an identity, to set it apart from other things. To "de-fine" something is to

The *Concept* of a Reasonable Christian Faith

apply a "fin", the Latin root for end, boundary. But such naming or defining places boundaries on a reality that is, without human interaction, un-named, un-defined, in-finite (no end, no boundaries). So human reality, according to Taoism, is a conceptualization, a limiting, of a reality that is always beyond it. To return to the idea of creating languages, a language is a process of dividing the world up into categories or concepts and applying names to the concepts. That's why different languages amount to different worldviews—each language is a different way of de-fining the experience of the people making the language.

This theory of language applies to religion as well. The world's religions were, by-and-large, started by individuals who had an experience of something that transcended the everyday world around them (Judaism, Christianity, Islam, and Buddhism all clearly exhibit this pattern). The difficulty, for these individuals, was to try to communicate their experience to the people around them. The only vehicle they had to communicate was their language. Now, if different languages are worldviews, then two people with two languages will have two worldviews. That means that the "names" (words, terms, concepts) they have to express their experience of the transcendent reality will be different. A "religion", then, is a conceptualization, a de-fining, a placing into language, of an experience of a reality that cannot, ultimately be captured by human language or human concepts. Here are some lines about religion from the *Tao Te Ching*:

> Now ritual is the husk of faith and loyalty, the beginning of confusion.
> Knowledge of the future is only a flowery trapping of the Tao.
> It is the beginning of folly.
>
> Therefore the truly great man dwells on what is real
> and not what is on the surface,
> On the fruit and not the flower,
> Therefore accepts the one and rejects the other.[25]

---

25. Tsu, *Tao Te Ching*, Chapter 38.

The rituals of a particular religion are, again, based on a human conceptualization of an ultimate reality—that's what I take "husk" to be referring to. They are the beginning of confusion because they are a particular conceptualization, which it is easy for practitioners to confuse for an actual display of the nature of the ultimate reality. The rituals dress up the conceptualization in "flowery trappings"—but while clothes dress things up, they hide what is beneath. The rituals are the surface, the flower, the clothes, but hide and can become confused with, the reality beneath. To take the particular conceptualization as the reality is "'the beginning of folly."

Several things follow from this theory. First, it lines up with and in fact predicts the fact that different groups of people, with different languages and cultures, will have different religions. Second, it implies that every religion is partly true and partly false. It is true insofar as it adequately reflects the character of the reality it is attempting to define. But it is false insofar as any human conceptualization or representation of the transcendent reality is a limitation and more-or-less a distortion of the unlimited character of that reality. This does not mean that every religion is as true as every other religion—there may be more or less accurate conceptualizations of the transcendent reality.

Christianity as Focus

Given that different religions are different conceptualizations of experiences of a transcendent reality, an important question is, is there any basis for evaluating different religions with respect to their conceptualization? There can't be an absolute way, because to compare a conceptualization with the reality would require us to be able to step outside of our conceptualization and compare it to the reality, which is impossible! Another possibility is that there is *no* way to make any evaluative comparisons, claiming that, since all religions are human conceptualizations, they are all equally accurate (or, better, equally inaccurate). I think that there is a path

The *Concept* of a Reasonable Christian Faith

in between these extremes. The world's major religions would be a good starting point.

I will focus my further discussion on Christianity, for several reasons. First, I have spent most of my life studying Christianity, directly and indirectly. In addition, Christianity is the dominant religion of North America, where I grew up and live. Third, Jesus' message is consistent with the limitations on what god must be like that I discussed earlier. Finally, I believe that Jesus has a particular message that addresses the concerns about faith and religion held by the New Atheists.

Interpreting Jesus

Interpreting Jesus is a notoriously difficult exercise. The first difficulty in interpreting him is that almost everything we know about him we know through the Gospels of the Christian Bible. Another difficulty is that Jesus and the accounts of him are 2000 years old and from a "pre-scientific" culture. Some people charge that because of these difficulties, the reports of the gospel writers about what Jesus said and did are biased and should not be trusted. However, I believe that this is a bad argument, and that it hides what is the real argument, which is also a bad argument. I believe the primary difficulty that modern people have in believing the gospels, which gives rise to the other two, is that Jesus did "miraculous" things. Scientific people (people who put an unreasonable weight on what can be known by the sciences) don't believe that miracles can happen, so they believe that any report of a miraculous event must be mistaken. If one believes that, then one can propose things like "the gospel writers were trying to propagate their beliefs" and "the gospel writers were pre-scientific people who didn't understand that miracles can't happen" in order to account for why the gospel writers claim that they experienced miraculous events in the company of Jesus. However, I believe that the argument for the main difficulty (scientism—see earlier discussion) is invalid, in which case there is no need for the explanations.

Once the possibility of miracles is granted (again, this is not to argue that miracles are common or to be expected; just that they are possible), the other challenges to the gospel accounts carry no weight. If it is possible that miracles can occur, there is another, simpler, explanation for why the Gospel writers reported experiencing miracles; it is that they were reporting what they in fact experienced. Similarly, the challenge that the gospel writers were "pre-scientific" only applies if it is already assumed that they didn't in fact experience miracles, based on the belief that miracles can't occur. If miracles can occur, then there is no reason to try to explain away the reports of miracles recorded by the gospel writers.

We must interpret the accounts about Jesus recorded by the gospel writers. The activity of interpreting texts is called "hermeneutics." I will use the term "hermeneutics of suspicion" to refer to a reading of the biblical texts with modern scientistic presuppositions (i.e., that miracles can't occur and that anything that doesn't fit with a modern scientific view of the world should be disbelieved). There is a problem with a hermeneutics of suspicion, though. It is, to re-use this fancy philosophical phrase, *self-referentially incoherent*. In order to have a hermeneutics of suspicion, you must be told about it. And you have to interpret the claims that are being told to you that lead you to adopt a hermeneutics of suspicion. And if you accept a hermeneutics of suspicion, you must be suspicious of any claim that doesn't fit neatly with a modern scientific view of the world. The problem is, "miracles can't occur" doesn't fit in with a modern scientific view of the world! As I have argued, science can't even address the status of miracles. To believe that miracles can't occur is not based on any science or any experience or observation. The result is that to accept a (scientific) hermeneutics of suspicion should lead one, rationally, to reject the hermeneutics of suspicion! Thus, a hermeneutics of suspicion refutes itself (this is what "self-referentially incoherent" means).

I propose here a different hermeneutics. I will call it an "open-minded hermeneutics." It is to approach texts carefully, but with an open mind. If the writer reports experiencing a miracle, it is reasonable to ask things like "did anyone else experience this?"

The *Concept* of a Reasonable Christian Faith

and "did this person have a history of mental illness?" and "was the person affected by drugs or alcohol at the time?" and "is the person known to fabricate stories?"[26] If none of the counter-explanations hold, then at some point the reasonable response to a report of a miracle is to believe that it happened. Given the number of miracles, the number of witnesses, the number of written reports, and the lack of evidence for any of these counter-explanations for the gospel reports of miracles, it is a reasonable response to believe that the reporters understood and accurately reported what they had experienced.

Jesus and God

If we read the gospel accounts about Jesus, he was (at least) a very remarkable person. He said remarkable things (some of which I will discuss shortly), and he did remarkable things. He performed miracles; turning water into wine, walking on water, healing sick people, raising people from the dead, and, finally, rising from the dead himself. It is not my intent to evaluate or discuss everything that Jesus said and did. My intent here is just to establish that, if Jesus said and did the kinds of things the gospel writers describe, he was a remarkable person. I would argue that he was the most remarkable human in recorded human history. If so, then it is worth thinking about what Jesus said and did, because we are likely to learn something from him. The core of what Jesus said and did was to claim to have a special relationship with God. Many books have been written regarding what the relationship between Jesus and God is or was, and, again, it is not my intention to enter that

---

26. David Hume famously argued that the probability that one of these things accounts for the report is always higher than the probability that a miracle has occurred. *An Enquiry Concerning Human Understanding*, Section X. This may be true, but doesn't, in itself, prove that a miracle hasn't occurred. Humans believe many things that are very improbable (for instance, anyone who has ever bought a lottery ticket is not too concerned with the rationality of probabilities). Probability arguments would also work against belief that life has arisen through natural processes on earth—the probability of that is very low.

debate. Whatever the specific relationship was, if we just look at what he said, Jesus himself claimed that he had a special relationship with God. So, it is likely that we can learn something about what God is like by examining what Jesus said and did. I will return to that task, but first I turn to a discussion of *faith*.

A REASONABLE CHRISTIAN *FAITH*

The writer of the New Testament book of Hebrews provides a very interesting definition of "faith." He writes, "Now faith is confidence about what we are hoping for, being convinced (as by evidence) of what is not seen."[27] At the outset, there is something paradoxical here—how can we be confident about something we are (only) hoping for? How can we be convinced, as by evidence, of what we can't see (with our eyes)?

Regarding confidence, that would depend on the trustworthiness of whoever promised what we are hoping for. To anticipate a later discussion, children of good, loving, parents will be very confident that their parents will follow through on what they have promised. The fact that parents have been good and loving in the past doesn't guarantee that they will continue to follow through on what's promised, but it makes it likely. In our context, the question becomes, how confident can we be that Jesus was an accurate demonstration of what God is like and what God wants from us? Part of faith is putting our trust in someone else. Trust and confidence are not all-or-nothing things. If we are certain of something, then no trust or confidence are involved. Religious faith is not certainty; it is being trusting and confident in the existence and character of a God without being absolutely certain. Can we put our trust in Jesus? I hope to show that it is at least not irrational to put our trust in him.

The next phrase in this definition is even more paradoxical—"being convinced (as by evidence) of what is not seen." The literal translation of the verb that I translate as "being convinced (as by

---

27. Heb 11:1. My own translation.

The *Concept* of a Reasonable Christian Faith

evidence)" is "a proof, that by which a thing is proved or tested." This is a very scientific, rational-sounding word. But how can something be proven without being seen? Not by scientific reasoning—that can only deal with what we see or experience through the senses (remember *empiricism*). Are there other ways of experience or "seeing" things? All of the world's religions claim that there is another way—some sort of "spiritual" seeing or experiencing. To support that Jesus meant something like this, I will mention two stories about Jesus.

In one story (which I will discuss in more detail later), Jesus meets a Samaritan woman at a well. They have a conversation in which he tells her facts about her life that he could not have known "empirically," since he had never met her before. She becomes convinced that he is the Messiah (god's special agent). At the end of the conversation, Jesus says "a time is coming—and now is here—when the true worshipers will worship the Father in spirit and truth, for the Father seeks such people to be his worshipers. God is spirit, and the people who worship him must worship in spirit and truth."[28] The juxtaposition of "spirit" and "truth" here is instructive. If we take "truth" to be a reference to empirical knowledge/experience/evidence, then Jesus is saying that there is a different kind of knowledge/experience/evidence in addition to the empirical kind. It's a "spiritual" kind. It's not clear what that means here, but there is a clear distinction being made. This distinction lines up well with the empiricist/rationalist distinction I discussed earlier. Empiricists tend to discount anything but empirical knowledge/experience/evidence, while rationalists seem to be open to non-empirical, maybe "spiritual," truth.

The other story is the story of Jesus and Nicodemus. It is worth reading:

> John 3:1–8 Now a certain man, a Pharisee named Nicodemus, who was a member of the Jewish ruling council, came to Jesus at night and said to him, "Rabbi, we know that you are a teacher who has come from God. For no one could perform the miraculous signs that you do unless God is

28. John 4:23–24.

> with him." Jesus replied, "I tell you the solemn truth, unless a person is born from above, he cannot see the kingdom of God." Nicodemus said to him, "How can a man be born when he is old? He cannot enter his mother's womb and be born a second time, can he?" Jesus answered, "I tell you the solemn truth, unless a person is born of water and spirit, he cannot enter the kingdom of God. What is born of the flesh is flesh, and what is born of the Spirit is spirit. Do not be amazed that I said to you, 'You must all be born from above.' The wind blows wherever it will, and you hear the sound it makes, but do not know where it comes from and where it is going. So it is with everyone who is born of the Spirit."

Notice the distinctions made here. "Born from above" (translated by many Christians as "born again") is being contrasted with "born from below (earth)", "born of water" is contrasted with "born of spirit", "born of the flesh" is contrasted with "born of the spirit." Also, note the claim by Jesus that "unless a person is born from above, they cannot see the kingdom of God." This is a strange use of the word "see", since all of the references to "spirit" are being contrasted with our physical self. How can we "see" non-physically, or "spiritually"? Whatever that means (and I confess that I don't really understand it and I have met almost no one who strikes me as having understood it), the distinction is clear, and the existence of such knowledge/experience/evidence is clear to Jesus.[29]

Faith is the assurance of things hoped for, the evidence of things not (empirically) seen. Faith is mysterious. It is different than reason, but connected. It seems to refer to accepting as true something that is not (empirically) proven. Is it ever reasonable to accept anything as true without full empirical proof? Several arguments support an affirmative answer. First, Jesus said that it is. Of course, this argument has some circularity, since faith is required to accept what Jesus said as true. Second, many very intelligent

---

29. The existence of non-empirical or spiritual knowledge is accepted by followers of every major world religion. The goal of Buddhist and Hindu meditation is to separate the mind from the senses and to "see" without reference to anything physical. This use of "see" is very similar to Jesus' use in this passage.

The *Concept* of a Reasonable Christian Faith

and rational people through history have said that it is. Finally, and perhaps most importantly, everyone has accepted a great deal of what they believe without full empirical proof. Common examples of such beliefs are the belief that someone who loves you actually loves you (they could be pretending), or the belief that Japan exists if you have never been there, or belief that there is or is not a God (since neither can be established empirically).

Part 2

The *Content* of a Reasonable Christian Faith

THE TWO IMAGES OF GOD

THE CHRISTIAN BIBLE SEEMS to present two images of God. One (found primarily in the Old Testament) is an angry, vindictive, punishing being (often combined under the term "holy"),[1] while the other is a loving, caring, merciful being. I believe that these images are inconsistent; that is, they cannot both be true. Even if one might argue that God is one way at one time and the other way at other times, or one way with some people and the other way with other people, these arguments introduce an inconsistency into God's nature that I find unacceptable. I think we have to work out which of these ways of being is true of God and which is not. And, as I argued earlier, if God is angry, vindictive, and punishing, then God is not worthy of our love or worship (even if it's in our best interest to follow what God says—but this is not to love or worship God). But I think there is good evidence that those are not the real

---

1. The Hebrew term "holy" means "set apart." God certainly is set apart from humans in terms of power and status, but being set apart does not in itself imply anger, vindictiveness, or being punishing. Even to include the notion of moral goodness in the connotation of "holiness" does not imply those characteristics. It, if anything, implies the opposite.

characteristics of God. Referring back to my discussion of Taoism, I take Jesus to be the best image we have of what God is like. Jesus' life, actions, and words will be my evidence.

WHAT IS GOD LIKE?

God the Father

In the Gospel of John, Jesus refers to God 129 times. In 72 of those references, he uses the phrase "the father"; in 25 of them he uses the phrase "my father"; and in 9, he speaks directly to God, calling him "Father." That accounts for 106 out of 129 references. In the other 23 references, he simply uses "God." I believe that looking at the way Jesus referred to God is instructive. The *only* term Jesus uses, other than "God", is "father."[2] Jesus himself then, understood God primarily as a father. I think this makes it reasonable to believe that God's primary characteristic is fatherhood.

With all analogies or metaphors, we have to think about what aspects of "father" Jesus had in mind. We all know there can be good fathers and bad fathers. And, in fact, fathers in the culture in which Jesus lived were often bad fathers (which fact I will discuss in a minute). The question then becomes, "what kind of father is God?" I assume we must take it that God is a good father. Then we have to wonder, "what is a good father?"

---

2. This data is supported by the Synoptic Gospels. In Mark (taken by many to be the oldest document), Jesus refers to God 39 times; he uses "God" in 31, and a form of "Father" in 4 (Mark also has him using "Lord" several times). In Matthew, taken by many to have used Mark or at least the document that Mark used, Jesus refers to God 67 times; he uses "God" 22 times and a form of "Father" in 34 (Matthew also has him using "Lord" several times). Luke has Jesus referring to God 77 times; he uses "God" 55 times and a form of "Father" 14 times (Luke also has him using "Lord" several times). While the references to "Father" are fewer in the Synoptics, "Father" and "Lord" are still the only terms used by Jesus other than "God", and "Father" is the most used term other than "God" in all of the accounts.

Patriarchy and Power

Jesus lived in a patriarchal culture. Generally, this means that men ruled. But there is another aspect of patriarchy that I think is deeper. Patriarchy means that men hold all of the *power*. I define *power* as "the ability to influence others." This applies to objects, like rocks and cars (known scientifically as "force") and to people. For people, we might divide power into two types; physical power; the ability to physically influence other people and things, and psychological power; the ability to motivate people to do things.

The problem with power for finite creatures in a finite world, as philosophers, theologians, and historians have stressed throughout history, is that it is always insecure. No matter how much power people accumulate, there is always the fear that a more powerful person will arise and take it (and likely destroy them in the process). So, life, for someone who is devoted to accumulating and maintaining power, is a never-ceasing effort to secure something that can never be secured absolutely.

Another noteworthy thing about power is that our power can never come close to God's power. If things are a matter of who has the most power, God wins without the slightest question. And God's power is not insecure; God is under no threat of losing God's power. So it would seem odd and inconsistent for God to make a world in which accumulation of power is the main objective. In my further discussion, I will use the term "the way of power" to refer to one possibility for the way God wants things to be in this world.

Jesus, Fathers, and Power

Since we are taking Jesus to have had an especially close relationship with and understanding of God, we can take it that Jesus has special insights into what God is like. Since we are taking God to be a good father, then we can take what Jesus says about God (and what Jesus does) to inform us of what God, the good father, is like. I will begin with some stories. The images of fathers in these stories challenge many of the cultural ideas about fathers and power

The *Content* of a Reasonable Christian Faith

at Jesus' time (and which continue in our time). In so doing, they lead us to reflect on the concepts of "good father" and "bad father," and they provide us with images of what it means to be a good father, as opposed to being a bad father. This is, to me, an indication of Jesus' brilliance and connection to God; he can take symbols that are well-known to us and use those symbols to connect to our concepts; but at the same transcend our understanding and teach us something new.

The Story of the Prodigal Son

Because these stories are so meaningful, I will reproduce the entire section:

> Luke 15:11-32 Then Jesus said, "A man had two sons. The younger of them said to his father, 'Father, give me the share of the estate that will belong to me.' So he divided his assets between them. After a few days, the younger son gathered together all he had and left on a journey to a distant country, and there he squandered his wealth with a wild lifestyle. Then after he had spent everything, a severe famine took place in that country, and he began to be in need. So he went and worked for one of the citizens of that country, who sent him to his fields to feed pigs. He was longing to eat the carob pods the pigs were eating, but no one gave him anything. But when he came to his senses he said, 'How many of my father's hired workers have food enough to spare, but here I am dying from hunger! I will get up and go to my father and say to him, "Father, I have sinned against heaven and against you. I am no longer worthy to be called your son; treat me like one of your hired workers."' So he got up and went to his father. But while he was still a long way from home his father saw him, and his heart went out to him; he ran and hugged his son and kissed him. Then his son said to him, 'Father, I have sinned against heaven and against you; I am no longer worthy to be called your son.' But the father said to his slaves, 'Hurry! Bring the best robe, and put it on him! Put a ring on his finger and sandals on his feet! Bring the

fattened calf and kill it! Let us eat and celebrate, because this son of mine was dead, and is alive again—he was lost and is found!' So they began to celebrate.

"Now his older son was in the field. As he came and approached the house, he heard music and dancing. So he called one of the slaves and asked what was happening. The slave replied, 'Your brother has returned, and your father has killed the fattened calf because he got his son back safe and sound.' But the older son became angry and refused to go in. His father came out and appealed to him, but he answered his father, 'Look! These many years I have worked like a slave for you, and I never disobeyed your commands. Yet you never gave me even a goat so that I could celebrate with my friends! But when this son of yours came back, who has devoured your assets with prostitutes, you killed the fattened calf for him!' Then the father said to him, 'Son, you are always with me, and everything that belongs to me is yours. It was appropriate to celebrate and be glad, for your brother was dead, and is alive; he was lost and is found.'"

A thorough and excellent presentation of the cultural context of the story of the prodigal son is presented by Kenneth Bailey in his book *Poet and Peasant*, and I will closely follow his remarks here.[3] Simply put, the events of the story would be quite remarkable to a first-century Jewish person. Perhaps the best way to understand the story is to hear it as it would have been expected to unfold by the people Jesus was talking to.

First century Israel, again, was a patriarchal culture. "Patriarchy", again, as I am using it, refers to a power-based culture in which the accumulation and preservation of power are the primary motivations. Fathers were the head of the household and had virtually limitless rights and power with respect to their households, including their wives and children. Women and children were expected to do what they were told and never challenge the position or authority (power) of the father. In that context, regarding the son's request for his share of the inheritance, Bailey says,

---

3. Bailey, *Poet and Peasant and Through Peasant Eyes: A Literary-Cultural Approach to the Parables in Luke (Combined edition).*

The *Content* of a Reasonable Christian Faith

> In over fifteen years I have been asking people of all walks of life from Morocco to India and from Turkey to the Sudan about the implications of a son's request for his inheritance while the father is still living. The answer has almost always been emphatically the same. I asked, "Has anyone ever made such a request in your village?" Response: "Never!" "Could anyone ever make such a request?" Response: "Impossible!" "If anyone ever did, what would happen?" Response: "His father would beat him, of course!" "Why?" Response: "This request means he wants his father to die!"[4]

To grant the boy's request, the father would have had to divide up his land and animals, sell the boy's portion (a third of the total for a second son) and give him the proceeds. This is a flagrant bid for power in a patriarchal system. The expected response of a patriarch would be clear—his power is being threatened; his primary motivation is protecting his power; so he would respond with aggression. He would beat the insolent child and send him away empty-handed and disinherited. The response by the father in the story is so unexpected that it would shock a patriarchal audience. The father does not respond with aggression or power-conservation. He willingly divests himself of his power and gives it to his son. This is not what power-mongers do! Something very unusual is going on here.

When the boy returns home, having lost all the money that he had been given, a patriarchal audience would again have had concrete expectations. In the case that a Jewish person lost all of his money to foreigners, the community would perform a *kezazah* ceremony, in which a clay pot would be broken to symbolize the permanently broken relationship between the community and the offender.[5] Regarding the tone of such a ceremony, Bailey writes,

> The father also knows how the village (which certainly has told him he should not have granted the inheritance in the first place) will treat the boy on his arrival. The

4. Bailey, *Poet and Peasant*, 161.
5. Bailey, *Poet and Peasant*, 167.

prodigal will be mocked by a crowd that will gather spontaneously as word flashes across the village telling of his return. An ancient writer, Ben Sirach, mentions four things in life that terrify him. Two of them are "slander by a whole town, and the gathering of a mob." The prodigal son returns to face both of Ben Sirach's terrors. The prodigal will be subject to taunt songs and many other types of verbal and perhaps even physical abuse.[6]

The response of the father, in such a situation, again, would be punishment and rejection. To lose your power in a power-conservation system is the ultimate shame. Not only has the boy lost his own power, but he has also thrown away his father's power. The father would have been justified in the eyes of the community, and expected, to join in the taunting and beating. The crowd would have been eagerly awaiting the thrashing this boy would receive from his father.

The father's response is unheard of to patriarchal ears. That he sees the boy at a distance and runs to him implies that he was going to save his boy from the mob that would gather as word spread of his return. In addition to going out to meet his son, the father's demeanor would have been unheard of. In a patriarchal culture, "face", or reputation is of utmost importance.[7] Patriarchs are proud, aloof, distant, and unemotional. Jewish men wore long robes. To run, the father would have had to hold up his robe and show his bare legs, which was humiliating (think of a contemporary Western man running in his underwear, or maybe even naked; that's how the Jewish culture of this time would have viewed the father). Again, the action of the father is so unexpected as to be shocking. The father is breaking all of the patriarchal, power-conservation rules. He is acting in ways that are shameful in the system. The audience hearing this story would have been flabbergasted.

When they meet and the son apologizes, the father again acts entirely uncharacteristically of a patriarch. The patriarch would

---

6. Bailey, *Poet and Peasant*, 181.

7. Bailey, *Poet and Peasant*, 130.

The *Content* of a Reasonable Christian Faith

have been aloof, angry, and aggressive. He would at least demand that the son grovel before him; more likely, as we have seen, he would have demanded that his son be beaten for his impudence and sent away. He would have demanded promises of eternal subjection from the son, with dire warnings about the extreme consequences (probably death) that would await him if he ever challenged the father's power again. But the father does none of these things. He doesn't even respond to the apology. He hugs and kisses the boy. He tells the servants to hurry with gifts and a celebration. The father restores him to his place in the family.

The level of meaning and depth in this story is remarkable. In it, Jesus addresses and transcends the culture in which he lives. He instructs the audience about the meaning of "true" or "good" fatherhood. Finally, he identifies the God whom he represents as just such a father. The audience (which included the religious leaders of Jerusalem) hearing this story must have been flabbergasted. The father's actions were so uncharacteristic of the culture that it is likely that people would have thought "this man has lost his sanity."

The actions of the father in this story, especially in its cultural context, imply some characteristics quite clearly. Regarding the boy's initial request, the father does not shame or punish or reject him, as a patriarch would have. He (quietly, in the story) grants the boy his freedom. This seems to indicate that good fathers (quietly) grant their children the freedom to challenge them, to explore, and to fail. By extension, Jesus is telling us that God (quietly) grants us the freedom to challenge him, to explore, and to fail. There is no anger portrayed here, no shaming, and no punishment.

Regarding the return of the boy, the story indicates that good fathers wait eagerly for their children who have left to return home; they run to meet them and accept them back with embarrassing emotional outpourings. They are not aloof, demanding, or unapproachable, as patriarchs are. This, again, is Jesus' description of what God is like. Again, there is no anger portrayed, no shaming, and no punishment.

The image of God as "good father" now gains some content. Good fathers are loving, open, passionate, forgiving, and merciful.

They place their relationships with their children above their personal, emotional, and social status; they are willing to look like fools to the people watching to establish and maintain those relationships. They welcome even children who have treated them very badly home with open arms, and give their (wayward) children parties and gifts when they return. There is no sign of judgment, vindictiveness, anger, or punishment here. That, says Jesus, is what good fathers and God are like.

It is an interesting question to wonder what would have happened if the son had never returned home. At least, the implication is that the father would have waited impatiently for the son's return. Would he have waited forever? I think the implication is that he would have, and never would the son be rejected or disallowed from returning.

This picture of fatherhood is expanded in another story.

The Story of the Father's Gifts

In his "Sermon on the Mount," Jesus says this about fathers:

> Matt 7:9-11 Is there anyone among you who, if his son asks for bread, will give him a stone? Or if he asks for a fish, will give him a snake? [And, from Luke 11:12 Or if he asks for an egg, will give him a scorpion?] If you then, although you are evil, know how to give good gifts to your children, how much more will your Father in heaven give good gifts to those who ask him!

In these three cases, the father is asked for something by the child; bread, a fish, and an egg. In each case the father gives the child something different; a stone, a snake, and a scorpion. Each of these examples involve the child asking for something necessary (food) and being given something unhelpful, and even harmful. What makes the examples even more disturbing is that in each case, the thing given by the father is similar to the thing asked for. The small loaves of bread used in this culture could be confused with a round stone. An eel or a snake might be mistaken for a

The *Content* of a Reasonable Christian Faith

fish. Scorpions can roll themselves into small balls that might be mistaken for an egg.[8] So the father is not only *not* giving the child something the child needs, the father is acting like he is giving the child what is needed, but, in reality, is potentially harming (or killing) the child.

As with the story of the prodigal son, this story is meant to shock us and make us reflect. We immediately respond; no parents would do such a thing to their child; no parents would give a child an unhelpful or harmful thing when asked for basic nourishment. But this is false; we hear stories of parents who neglect and abuse their children all the time, so would the people who were hearing the story. And if we take "nourishment" in a more figurative sense, it gets worse. How many times do your and my children ask for our time and love and attention and we give them poor substitutes for those things? I do it all too often. How many stories do we hear of parents who actively harm their children? But we all recognize that that is not what an ideal parent does. Jesus' point is that if we, being less than ideal, understand what it means to give good things to our children, how much more will God, who is a perfectly good parent, give us what we need when we ask for it?

I believe that there is a further criticism of patriarchy in this story. Patriarchal fathers, as we have seen, are characterized by distance, aloofness, judgmentalness, and anger. But these are all the opposite of what children need to grow and develop healthily. I believe Jesus is telling his audience (and us), again, that patriarchy and power-conservation are not part of good parenting or characteristics of God.

Some people may immediately respond that they have asked God for things and have not gotten any reply at all—I am sympathetic to this objection and will talk about it more later. But, at least, Jesus' idea is clear. A good father is one who gives his children what they need and doesn't give unhelpful or harmful substitutes for what his children need.

---

8. For examples, see http://biblehub.com/commentaries/matthew/7-10.htm.

A Reasonable Christian Faith

God's Words About Jesus

Another clue about good fathers comes from two reports in the gospels of God speaking about Jesus. The first one happens after Jesus is baptized by John, and the second one is in the account called "the transfiguration":

> Matt 3:16–17 *After Jesus was baptized, just as he was coming up out of the water, the heavens opened and he saw the Spirit of God descending like a dove and coming on him. And a voice from heaven said, "This is my beloved Son; in him I take great delight."*

> Matt 17:1–5 *Six days later Jesus took with him Peter, James, and John the brother of James, and led them privately up a high mountain. And he was transfigured before them. His face shone like the sun, and his clothes became white as light. Then Moses and Elijah also appeared before them, talking with him. So Peter said to Jesus, "Lord, it is good for us to be here. If you want, I will make three shelters—one for you, one for Moses, and one for Elijah." While he was still speaking, a bright cloud overshadowed them, and a voice from the cloud said, "This is my beloved Son, in whom I take great delight. Listen to him!"*

I want to note several things about God's words. First, God uses the word "beloved" to describe Jesus in both cases. The Greek word here is "agapatos," based on "agape." I'll have more to say about this term later, but it means "love" with a particular sense. Second, God says, to reword slightly, "I am delighted with my son." So in the only two direct statements by God, God loves and is delighted with his son.

Fathers and Anger

God is commonly portrayed as angry, especially in conservative and fundamentalist Christian churches. Is this an accurate portrayal of God? I would like to examine that picture, based on the

The *Content* of a Reasonable Christian Faith

thesis that Jesus' primary image of God as a good father. Are good fathers angry?

It seems to me that I am angry at my children for a number of reasons. Most of them are bad reasons. One of the main times that I am angry is when I am tired. When I am tired, my patience is short and when my children don't do things exactly how I want them to, I become frustrated and angry. Is this positive? It seems to me that it isn't. If I were better rested, I would feel more patient, and if I felt more patient I would respond to my children without anger. But God, according to the Bible, doesn't suffer from tiredness or impatience, so it is unlikely that God would be angry for those reasons. And it seems that we could say that there is an inverse relationship between this kind of anger and goodness in fathering; that is, the more impatient anger a father directs at his children, the less likely it is that he is being a good father.

I also get angry when my children disobey me. But I don't think this is healthy anger. Why would disobedience cause me to be angry? It seems like it's the challenge to my authority or power or control (which are all really the same issue) that makes me angry. But to respond to a challenge with anger is related to fear and insecurity; ultimately, fear that I will lose my authority or power, which implies that I am not secure in my authority or power. Again, a lot of conservative Christians say that God gets angry when we disobey him. But God is infinitely powerful; why would he be insecure or fearful about losing his power? The Prodigal Son story is precisely a story of a father having his authority challenged. The main point of that story is that the father *didn't* react angrily. I think there's no reason to believe that God is angry at disobedience. Again, we might say, the more a father is angry at disobedience, the less good the father is.

There is one form of anger that seems positive. One day, my daughter was holding a guinea pig that we were watching for the weekend. The guinea pig pooped on her hand. She screamed and threw the guinea pig several feet into its cage. This made me very angry, and I yelled angrily at her. In this case, I think my anger was warranted, because I was protecting an innocent, weaker, being from being harmed by a much larger, more powerful being. It seems like God could be angry in this sense. In fact, as I will show later on, Jesus displays just this kind of anger.

WHAT DOES GOD WANT FROM US?

I am taking "good father" or "good parent" as the basic descriptor of God. A further question is, "what does God want from us?" Relative to God, we are children. One of the ideas that I have already considered is that good parents give children what they (really) need. What do children need? To answer that question, I want to reflect on what it is like to be a child. I think that children are primarily weak, ignorant, insecure persons. Children have very limited knowledge, power or resources and they live in a big, unfamiliar, frightening, and dangerous world. So, I take it that the primary status of children is insecurity.

What do (relatively) secure, good parents want from and for their insecure children? In a word, security. They want *for* their children to be safe and to have the resources to grow up to be healthy, mature, happy adults. They want *from* their children to play, to learn, to act like children, to enter into healthy relationships, and love (agape) people around them.

As I said earlier, I take Jesus to be the highest and best representation that humans have experienced of what God is like and what God wants from us. So, in addition to the direct references to God that we have considered so far, we can look at what Jesus himself said and did as representations of what God is like and what God wants from us. I will now turn to look at Jesus' actions and words.

What did Jesus say and do?

When Jesus announced the beginning of his ministry, he used this quotation from Isaiah: "The Spirit of the Lord is upon me, because he has anointed me to proclaim good news to the poor. He has sent

The *Content* of a Reasonable Christian Faith

me to proclaim release to the captives and the regaining of sight to the blind, to set free those who are oppressed, to proclaim the year of the Lord's favor" (Luke 4:18–19). The problem(s) that Jesus came to address, according to him, were captivity (physical, economic, mental, or spiritual), poverty (physical, economic, mental, or spiritual), blindness (physical, economic, mental, or spiritual), and oppression (physical, economic, mental, or spiritual). He was not arriving with bad news of judgment for people; he was arriving with good news. He was not here to announce God's *disfavor* with captive, poor, blind, oppressed people, but God's *favor*. This is not a message of anger and punishment, but one of support and help. This message is entirely consistent with our model of God as a good parent. At whom is this message directed? It's clear to me that the extension of these types includes everybody. The common element in all these types of Jesus refers to is insecurity. So we could say, according to Jesus, his message is to proclaim hope to the insecure (everyone).

The Samaritan woman at the well

Perhaps my favorite story about Jesus is the story about him meeting a Samaritan woman at a well. Here is the text, from the book of John:

> *John 4:4–30 But [Jesus] had to pass through Samaria. Now he came to a Samaritan town called Sychar, near the plot of land that Jacob had given to his son Joseph. Jacob's well was there, so Jesus, since he was tired from the journey, sat right down beside the well. It was about noon.*
>
> *A Samaritan woman came to draw water. Jesus said to her, "Give me some water to drink." (For his disciples had gone off into the town to buy supplies.) So the Samaritan woman said to him, "How can you—a Jew—ask me, a Samaritan woman, for water to drink?" (For Jews use nothing in common with Samaritans.)*
>
> *Jesus answered her, "If you had known the gift of God and who it is who said to you, 'Give me some water to drink,' you would have asked him, and he would have*

given you living water." "Sir," the woman said to him, "you have no bucket and the well is deep; where then do you get this living water? Surely you're not greater than our ancestor Jacob, are you? For he gave us this well and drank from it himself, along with his sons and his livestock."

Jesus replied, "Everyone who drinks some of this water will be thirsty again. But whoever drinks some of the water that I will give him will never be thirsty again, but the water that I will give him will become in him a fountain of water springing up to eternal life." The woman said to him, "Sir, give me this water, so that I will not be thirsty or have to come here to draw water." He said to her, "Go call your husband and come back here." The woman replied, "I have no husband." Jesus said to her, "Right you are when you said, 'I have no husband,' for you have had five husbands, and the man you are living with now is not your husband. This you said truthfully!"

The woman said to him, "Sir, I see that you are a prophet. Our fathers worshiped on this mountain, and you people say that the place where people must worship is in Jerusalem." Jesus said to her, "Believe me, woman, a time is coming when you will worship the Father neither on this mountain nor in Jerusalem. You people worship what you do not know. We worship what we know, because salvation is from the Jews. But a time is coming—and now is here—when the true worshipers will worship the Father in spirit and truth, for the Father seeks such people to be his worshipers. God is spirit, and the people who worship him must worship in spirit and truth." The woman said to him, "I know that Messiah is coming" (the one called Christ); "whenever he comes, he will tell us everything." Jesus said to her, "I, the one speaking to you, am he."

Now at that very moment his disciples came back. They were shocked because he was speaking with a woman. However, no one said, "What do you want?" or "Why are you speaking with her?" Then the woman left her water jar, went off into the town and said to the people, "Come, see a man who told me everything I ever did. Surely he can't be the Messiah, can he?" So they left the town and began coming to him.

The *Content* of a Reasonable Christian Faith

The first thing to note about this passage was the person with whom Jesus was speaking; a Samaritan woman. The cultural mandate for (male) Jews of Jesus' time with respect to Samaritans and women cannot be made more clear than this quotation from the Mishnah: "the daughters of the Samaritans are menstruants from their cradle."[9] A Samaritan (non-Jewish) woman (non-male) was doubly culturally unapproachable for a Jewish male. For Jesus to talk to her openly, and even worse, to drink from her water jar, was unthinkable. The woman shows her shock by asking him what basis he had for addressing her, and the disciples are similarly shocked when they return and find him talking to her.

Showing her shock, the woman asked Jesus, "How can you—a Jew—ask me, a Samaritan woman, for water to drink?" Jesus does not answer her question but notes that he has a different kind of water, "living water," that she should be asking him for. Not understanding, she points out that the well is deep and he has no bucket. Jesus again answers mysteriously, talking about the merits of his "living water." The woman, who is also courageous and counter-cultural to enter the conversation, is intrigued and asks for some of Jesus' water.

In the really fascinating part of the conversation, Jesus again changes the topic and asks her to go get her husband. When she replies (semi-honestly) that she doesn't have a husband, Jesus tells her something that he could not have known naturally (if readers doesn't believe that anything non-natural can happen, they will have to account for this response some other way; but the woman's response is clearly the response of someone who believed that Jesus couldn't have known this information).

The woman now changes the subject and they talk about worshipping God (there is another reference here to worshipping "in spirit and in truth," which I have discussed with respect to the concepts of faith and reason). But that is not the part of the story that I want to discuss. The point I want to focus is on is that, when

---

9. Mishnah Niddah 4.1, quoted in David Daube, "The Meaning of συγχραομαι."

the woman changes the subject, Jesus does not press the issue of her relational status.

Note what Jesus has done. He has approached a person who is culturally off limits. Not only is she culturally off limits, she is living outside of the moral and religious boundaries of Judaism (and probably any other culture). By Jewish law, she is objectively "sinful." (Female) Sexual non-conformity is treated very harshly by patriarchal cultures. Some commentators on this passage even state that the fact that she is at the well at noon is a sign that she didn't want to be there in the morning, when the sexually conforming women drew their water, because of the gossip and rejection she would experience in their presence.

Jesus, again, doesn't dwell on or mention the woman's sexual status. He just offers her "living (spiritual) water." When he brings it up, he says nothing like "you have to go and become sexually conforming before you can have this spiritual water." He also doesn't say "if I give you this water, you'll have to become sexually conforming." The offer of spiritual water has no conditions. Jesus makes clear that he knows her and her situation, but he pointedly does not mention her changing in any way as a condition of or a response to his offer. This is consistent with our model of God as the good parent. If the children of good parents are having difficulty with something or doing something that the parents don't think is good for them, good parents don't become angry and vindictive and punishing; they offer help and assistance. They don't view their children as "bad" or "sinful", they view them as weak, ignorant, limited persons, trying to achieve the most happiness they can within the situation in which they find themselves. This is again consistent with Jesus self-introduction as a deliverer from (cultural and social) oppression.

Agape

In one of many confrontations with the religious leaders, Jesus had this conversation:

The *Content* of a Reasonable Christian Faith

> *Matt 22:34–40 Now when the Pharisees heard that he had silenced the Sadducees, they assembled together. And one of them, an expert in religious law, asked him a question to test him: "Teacher, which commandment in the law is the greatest?" Jesus said to him, "'Love the Lord your God with all your heart, with all your soul, and with all your mind.' This is the first and greatest commandment. The second is like it: 'Love your neighbor as yourself.' All the law and the prophets depend on these two commandments."*

"The law" that the religious leaders are referring to is the complex set of religious, moral, and social laws of the Jewish Scriptures (the Torah, or what Christians call the Old Testament). Jesus acts according to the Tao; he moves beyond the trappings of the ritual to the underlying reality. The basis of law is love.

The Greek word translated "love" here is the (in)famous term "agape." Much has been written about this term; I want just to get a basic definition and see where else Jesus uses it. Strong's Concordance defines it as "affection, good-will, love, benevolence." As a reminder, the word "agape" is used in the two records of God speaking about Jesus, when he calls him his "beloved son." So, part of Jesus' and command to love each other is to love as God (the father) loves Jesus (the son).

"Agape" means more than just a sentiment or feeling. In what is perhaps the most famous of all Bible verses, John 3:16, the word "agape" is used as well. "For this is the way God loved [agape] the world: He gave his one and only Son, so that everyone who believes in him will not perish but have eternal life." This verse adds to the meaning; to love is to be so interested in the good of the other as to be willing to give things that are good for the receiver, even sacrificially (this further informs our understanding of being a good parent).

Another instructive—and difficult—use of "agape" by Jesus is in the Sermon on the Mount:

> *Matt 5:43–46 "You have heard that it was said, 'Love your neighbor' and 'hate your enemy.' But I say to you, love your enemy and pray for those who persecute you, so that you*

> *may be like your father in heaven, since he causes the sun to rise on the evil and the good, and sends rain on the righteous and the unrighteous. For if you love those who love you, what reward do you have? Even the tax collectors do the same, don't they?"*

Here the command to love is extended not only to those close to us, with whom we get along. We are commanded to act for the good of the other even when the other is our enemy.

Jesus claims in yet another spot (all the uses of "love" here are instances of "agape"):

> *John 15:9-13 "Just as the father has loved me, I have also loved you; remain in my love. If you obey my commandments, you will remain in my love, just as I have obeyed my father's commandments and remain in his love. I have told you these things so that my joy may be in you, and your joy may be complete. My commandment is this—to love one another just as I have loved you. No one has greater love than this—that one lays down his life for his friends."*

Interestingly, here we have an equation of commands, obedience, and love. Jesus obeys his father's command and asks his followers to follow his command—but the command itself is love (sacrificially), nothing else.

Let us, then, construct a working definition of "agape," which we are translating as "love." I suggest to use this: "to love someone is to care about their good to the extent that we are willing to act (even sacrificially) to bring that good about."

I want to make one clarification about love. Many people, especially parents, claim to be doing things out of love, when it is pretty obvious to everyone else that it is not love that is motivating them—it is the good of the one "loving" that is really at stake, disguised as seeking the good of the other. I take it as a necessary component of love that people understand (through education) what is actually good for other people, and test their "love" to make sure it conforms to this requirement.

We are to love God, ourselves, and others (even if they are enemies). As a side note, I believe we either succeed or fail at all

The *Content* of a Reasonable Christian Faith

of these at the same time—we can't love God without loving ourselves and others, we can't love ourselves without loving God and others, and we can't love others without loving God and ourselves.

Fruit

Jesus talks a lot about "fruit." Here are some of the passages:

> *Matt 7:15-20 (also Luke 6:43) "Watch out for false prophets, who come to you in sheep's clothing but inwardly are voracious wolves. You will recognize them by their fruit. Grapes are not gathered from thorns or figs from thistles, are they? In the same way, every good tree bears good fruit, but the bad tree bears bad fruit. A good tree is not able to bear bad fruit, nor a bad tree to bear good fruit. Every tree that does not bear good fruit is cut down and thrown into the fire. So then, you will recognize them by their fruit.*

> *Matt 12:33-35 "Make a tree good and its fruit will be good, or make a tree bad and its fruit will be bad, for a tree is known by its fruit. Offspring of vipers! How are you able to say anything good, since you are evil? For the mouth speaks from what fills the heart. The good person brings good things out of his good treasury, and the evil person brings evil things out of his evil treasury.*

> *Matt 13:18-23 (also Luke 8:11 and Mark 4:13) "So listen to the parable of the sower: When anyone hears the word about the kingdom and does not understand it, the evil one comes and snatches what was sown in his heart; this is the seed sown along the path. The seed sown on rocky ground is the person who hears the word and immediately receives it with joy. But he has no root in himself and does not endure; when trouble or persecution comes because of the word, immediately he falls away. The seed sown among thorns is the person who hears the word, but worldly cares and the seductiveness of wealth choke the word, so it produces nothing. But as for the seed sown on good soil, this is the person who hears the word and understands. He bears fruit, yielding a hundred, sixty, or thirty times what was sown."*

Matt 21:43 [to the Scribes] For this reason I tell you that the kingdom of God will be taken from you and given to a people who will produce its fruit.

Luke 3:7-14 [John speaking, not Jesus] Even now the ax is laid at the root of the trees, and every tree that does not produce good fruit will be cut down and thrown into the fire." So the crowds were asking him, "What then should we do?" John answered them, "The person who has two tunics must share with the person who has none, and the person who has food must do likewise." Tax collectors also came to be baptized, and they said to him, "Teacher, what should we do?" He told them, "Collect no more than you are required to." Then some soldiers also asked him, "And as for us—what should we do?" He told them, "Take money from no one by violence or by false accusation, and be content with your pay."

Luke 13:6-9 Then Jesus told this parable: "A man had a fig tree planted in his vineyard, and he came looking for fruit on it and found none. So he said to the worker who tended the vineyard, 'For three years now, I have come looking for fruit on this fig tree, and each time I inspect it I find none. Cut it down! Why should it continue to deplete the soil?' But the worker answered him, 'Sir, leave it alone this year too, until I dig around it and put fertilizer on it. Then if it bears fruit next year, very well, but if not, you can cut it down.'"

John 15:1-17 "I am the true vine and my Father is the gardener. He takes away every branch that does not bear fruit in me. He prunes every branch that bears fruit so that it will bear more fruit. You are clean already because of the word that I have spoken to you. Remain in me, and I will remain in you. Just as the branch cannot bear fruit by itself, unless it remains in the vine, so neither can you unless you remain in me. "I am the vine; you are the branches. The one who remains in me—and I in him—bears much fruit, because apart from me you can accomplish nothing. If anyone does not remain in me, he is thrown out like a branch, and dries up; and such branches are gathered up and thrown into the fire, and are burned up. If you remain

The *Content* of a Reasonable Christian Faith

in me and my words remain in you, ask whatever you want, and it will be done for you. My Father is honored by this, that you bear much fruit and show that you are my disciples. "Just as the Father has loved me, I have also loved you; remain in my love. If you obey my commandments, you will remain in my love, just as I have obeyed my Father's commandments and remain in his love. I have told you these things so that my joy may be in you, and your joy may be complete. My commandment is this—to love one another just as I have loved you. No one has greater love than this—that one lays down his life for his friends. You are my friends if you do what I command you. I no longer call you slaves, because the slave does not understand what his master is doing. But I have called you friends, because I have revealed to you everything I heard from my Father. You did not choose me, but I chose you and appointed you to go and bear fruit, fruit that remains, so that whatever you ask the Father in my name he will give you. This I command you—to love one another.

"Fruit" is obviously a metaphor in these passages—Jesus isn't telling us to grow grapes! Metaphors always require interpretation. "Bearing fruit" is clearly a metaphor for producing something, and Jesus seems pretty adamant about the necessity for his followers to be producing "fruit"—but what is it? Conservative Christians often interpret "bearing fruit'" as "winning souls" or "witnessing to non-believers" (usually in a harsh and judgmental way), but I think that is a misinterpretation.

Two of the passages I cited provide an indication of what "fruit" refers to. In the Luke 3:7 passage, although it is John speaking, after he mentions fruit, the listeners ask "what should we do?" John responds, "The person who has two tunics must share with the person who has none, and the person who has food must do likewise;" "Collect no more [taxes] than you are required to;" and "Take money from no one by violence or by false accusation, and be content with your pay." None of these commands mention "believing in Jesus" or "witnessing" at all. They have to do with how we treat the people around us; they all fit our definition of "love."

The connection between fruit and love is strengthened by Jesus' word in the John 15 passage. This is an extended metaphor about Jesus being the vine and we being the branches of the vine that are (or are not) bearing fruit. There is a very interesting connection of ideas; "If you obey my commandments, you will remain in my love, just as I have obeyed my Father's commandments and remain in his love . . . My commandment is this—to love one another just as I have loved you." Jesus and his Father love (agape) each other and Jesus obeys the Father's commands. This is a model for us; fruit is connected to love, which is connected to commands. But Jesus specifically states the command twice in the passage—the command is to love each other (which is supported by Jesus' statement of the greatest commandment—to love God, others, and ourselves). So in the end, fruit is love.

The interpretation of "fruit" as love is further strengthened by the (in)famous passage in Matthew about the sheep and the goats:

> Matt 25:31-45 "When the Son of Man comes in his glory and all the angels with him, then he will sit on his glorious throne. All the nations will be assembled before him, and he will separate people one from another like a shepherd separates the sheep from the goats. He will put the sheep on his right and the goats on his left. Then the king will say to those on his right, 'Come, you who are blessed by my Father, inherit the kingdom prepared for you from the foundation of the world. For I was hungry and you gave me food, I was thirsty and you gave me something to drink, I was a stranger and you invited me in, I was naked and you gave me clothing, I was sick and you took care of me, I was in prison and you visited me.' Then the righteous will answer him, 'Lord, when did we see you hungry and feed you, or thirsty and give you something to drink? When did we see you a stranger and invite you in, or naked and clothe you? When did we see you sick or in prison and visit you?' And the king will answer them, 'I tell you the truth, just as you did it for one of the least of these brothers or sisters of mine, you did it for me.'
>
> "Then he will say to those on his left, 'Depart from me, you accursed, into the eternal fire that has been prepared

The *Content* of a Reasonable Christian Faith

> *for the devil and his angels! For I was hungry and you gave me nothing to eat, I was thirsty and you gave me nothing to drink. I was a stranger and you did not receive me as a guest, naked and you did not clothe me, sick and in prison and you did not visit me.' Then they too will answer, 'Lord, when did we see you hungry or thirsty or a stranger or naked or sick or in prison, and did not give you whatever you needed?' Then he will answer them, 'I tell you the truth, just as you did not do it for one of the least of these, you did not do it for me.' 25:46 And these will depart into eternal punishment, but the righteous into eternal life."*

This passage is about salvation, and I find it instructive that "belief" in Jesus is not mentioned in the passage. But the actions mentioned in the passage line up with the interpretation that when Jesus talks about "bearing fruit," he is talking about loving the people around us, especially the hungry and enslaved ones (as he announced was his own mission).

As one final basis for interpreting "fruit," I will step outside of the gospels, because this passage is clear and helpful. Paul, in his letter to the Galatians (5:22–23), says "But the fruit of the Spirit is love, joy, peace, patience, kindness, goodness, faithfulness, gentleness, and self-control. Against such things there is no law." If we want to look at fruit as the development of a certain way of interacting with the world around us, this is an excellent (and sobering) list of personality traits to use for self-evaluation.

Forgiveness

Forgiveness is mentioned by Jesus many times in the gospels. It is worth taking the time to read some of the passages.

> Matt 6:9–14 So pray this way:
>
> > Our Father in heaven, may your name be honored,
> > may your kingdom come,
> > may your will be done on earth as it is in heaven.
> > Give us today our daily bread,
> > and forgive us our debts, as we ourselves have forgiven

our debtors.
And do not lead us into temptation, but deliver us from the evil one.
For if you forgive others their sins, your heavenly Father will also forgive you. But if you do not forgive others, your Father will not forgive you your sins.

Matt 18:23-35 "For this reason, the kingdom of heaven is like a king who wanted to settle accounts with his slaves. As he began settling his accounts, a man who owed ten thousand talents was brought to him. Because he was not able to repay it, the lord ordered him to be sold, along with his wife, children, and whatever he possessed, and repayment to be made. Then the slave threw himself to the ground before him, saying, 'Be patient with me, and I will repay you everything.' The lord had compassion on that slave and released him, and forgave him the debt. After he went out, that same slave found one of his fellow slaves who owed him one hundred silver coins. So he grabbed him by the throat and started to choke him, saying, 'Pay back what you owe me!' Then his fellow slave threw himself down and begged him, 'Be patient with me, and I will repay you.' But he refused. Instead, he went out and threw him in prison until he repaid the debt. When his fellow slaves saw what had happened, they were very upset and went and told their lord everything that had taken place. Then his lord called the first slave and said to him, 'Evil slave! I forgave you all that debt because you begged me! Should you not have shown mercy to your fellow slave, just as I showed it to you?' And in anger his lord turned him over to the prison guards to torture him until he repaid all he owed. So also my heavenly Father will do to you, if each of you does not forgive your brother from your heart."

Luke 6:37-38 "Do not judge, and you will not be judged; do not condemn, and you will not be condemned; forgive, and you will be forgiven. Give, and it will be given to you: A good measure, pressed down, shaken together, running over, will be poured into your lap. For the measure you use will be the measure you receive."

The *Content* of a Reasonable Christian Faith

One of the clear themes in these passages is that being forgiven by God for what we have done or how we have lived is contingent on our willingness to forgive others for what they have done (especially to us). This is an extremely demanding condition. I find it extremely difficult to forgive people who have wronged me. My sense of self-righteousness in such cases is strong—I want the other people to grovel, to beg, to subject themselves to me. But this is to act in the Way of Power. These are all efforts to regain power by taking it from someone else. Whatever someone has done to me, it can't be undone, even if they grovel and beg for forgiveness.

The question of what it means to forgive someone is a difficult question. If someone has murdered someone close to me, am I to forget that it happened? If a person is being abused by a partner, and each time, the offending partner begs for forgiveness, is the abused partner required to remain with the abuser? I want to propose a definition of "forgive" and then offer several observations regarding how it could be applied.

I take "to forgive" to mean "ceasing to view the other person in terms of blame and shame, and ceasing to allow another person to have a negative effect on oneself." To answer the earlier questions about forgiveness, to forgive does not mean to forget that something happened. It does not mean not to protect ourselves from another person or not to separate ourselves from another person. It means not to view the other person in terms of judgment, shame and punishment.

Judgment

The flip side of forgiveness is judgment. Jesus also discusses judgment often. Here are some samples:

> Matt 7:1-5 *"Do not judge so that you will not be judged. For by the standard you judge you will be judged, and the measure you use will be the measure you receive. Why do you see the speck in your brother's eye, but fail to see the beam of wood in your own? Or how can you say to your brother, 'Let me remove the speck from your eye,' while*

there is a beam in your own? You hypocrite! First remove the beam from your own eye, and then you can see clearly to remove the speck from your brother's eye."

Matt 5:21-26 "You have heard that it was said to an older generation, 'Do not murder,' and 'whoever murders will be subjected to judgment.' But I say to you that anyone who is angry with a brother will be subjected to judgment. And whoever insults a brother will be brought before the council, and whoever says 'Fool' will be sent to fiery hell. So then, if you bring your gift to the altar and there remember that your brother has something against you, leave your gift there in front of the altar. First go and be reconciled to your brother and then come and present your gift. Reach agreement quickly with your accuser while on the way to court, or he may hand you over to the judge, and the judge hand you over to the warden, and you will be thrown into prison. I tell you the truth, you will never get out of there until you have paid the last penny!"

Luke 6:37-38 "Do not judge, and you will not be judged; do not condemn, and you will not be condemned; forgive, and you will be forgiven. Give, and it will be given to you: A good measure, pressed down, shaken together, running over, will be poured into your lap. For the measure you use will be the measure you receive."

In the first, hyperbolic, passage, Jesus is very clear about what God thinks of people judging other people's lives and actions: we will be judged by God by the same criteria that we use to judge others. The principle behind the speck-and-beam analogy is evident in the world around me. My children are quick to cry foul when their sibling does the very thing they were just excusing themselves for doing. Sports fans are quick to question the call of a referee when they supported the same call against the opposing team. Politicians and the news media distort and condemn the policies and actions of the other party but excuse similar actions and policies in their own party. We seem to have a propensity to ignore the beams in our own eyes while we are busy condemning the specks we notice in others'.

The *Content* of a Reasonable Christian Faith

Recall the story of the woman at the well, who was living a "sinful" life. Jesus did not condemn or judge her—he offered her living water with no strings attached. The question of her future actions did not even arise in the conversation.

The second and third passages are equally strong. The message is clear—we have no basis for making judgments about the spiritual status of any other person, on pain of having the same criterion applied to us. This message, more than anything else Jesus said, frightens me! It makes me want to be exceedingly loving, forgiving, and non-judgmental in my treatment of others.

Anger (again) - Jesus and the Pharisees

The question of God being angry arose earlier; I want to consider it again. In the following passages, Jesus is talking to the "experts in the law" and the Pharisees, the religious leaders of his time.

> *Matt 23:1-7 Then Jesus said to the crowds and to his disciples, "The experts in the law and the Pharisees sit on Moses' seat. Therefore pay attention to what they tell you and do it. But do not do what they do, for they do not practice what they teach. They tie up heavy loads, hard to carry, and put them on men's shoulders, but they themselves are not willing even to lift a finger to move them. They do all their deeds to be seen by people, for they make their phylacteries wide and their tassels long. They love the place of honor at banquets and the best seats in the synagogues and elaborate greetings in the marketplaces, and to have people call them 'Rabbi.'"*

Jesus is quite clear about his concerns with the religious leaders (they equally apply to political leaders; maybe leaders of any sort). They pile heavy loads on people's shoulders, they dress in fancy clothes while the people around them are in poverty, they like to have the best seats at gatherings. But these are all aspects of the Way of Power, not the Way of Love. The religious leaders are trying to gain power and status at the expense of the people around them, without helping the people they are supposed to be helping. In the next few verses Jesus' words become angry.

> Matt 23:15-27 "Woe to you, experts in the law and you Pharisees, hypocrites! You cross land and sea to make one convert, and when you get one, you make him twice as much a child of hell as yourselves! . . .
>
> "Woe to you, experts in the law and you Pharisees, hypocrites! You give a tenth of mint, dill, and cumin, yet you neglect what is more important in the law—justice, mercy, and faithfulness! You should have done these things without neglecting the others. Blind guides! You strain out a gnat yet swallow a camel!
>
> "Woe to you, experts in the law and you Pharisees, hypocrites! You clean the outside of the cup and the dish, but inside they are full of greed and self-indulgence. Blind Pharisee! First clean the inside of the cup, so that the outside may become clean too!
>
> "Woe to you, experts in the law and you Pharisees, hypocrites! You are like whitewashed tombs that look beautiful on the outside but inside are full of the bones of the dead and of everything unclean. In the same way, on the outside you look righteous to people, but inside you are full of hypocrisy and lawlessness."

Jesus is expressing a great deal of anger at these religious leaders. But note, first, at whom he is angry. It's people who claim to be religious but don't act the way God wants people to act—he calls them "hypocrites" a number of times.[10] Note also what his complaints are. They are about the religious leaders focusing on their appearance and their status and their powerful positions, rather than doing what they are supposed to be doing; bringing God and the people together (remember Taoism and the folly of ritual). Jesus accuses them of not loving—of making life more difficult for the people they were supposed to be serving, rather than less difficult (verse 4). I think Jesus is primarily angry at more powerful

---

10. The Greek word "hupokrites" "was commonly used of actors on the Greek stage" (https://biblehub.com/greek/5273). It refers to people who wear a mask; who act one way on the surface, but are really something different beneath.

people protecting and increasing their power at the expense of less powerful people. Remember the story about the good fathers' gifts to his children? The religious leaders are doing just what the bad fathers do in the story; people ask them for basic (spiritual) sustenance, and they give them poisonous substitutes for spirituality.

Similarly, look at this passage in which Jesus talks about children:

> Matt 18:1-6 *At that time the disciples came to Jesus saying, "Who is the greatest in the kingdom of heaven?" He called a child, had him stand among them, and said, "I tell you the truth, unless you turn around and become like little children, you will never enter the kingdom of heaven! Whoever then humbles himself like this little child is the greatest in the kingdom of heaven. And whoever welcomes a child like this in my name welcomes me. But if anyone causes one of these little ones who believe in me to sin, it would be better for him to have a huge millstone hung around his neck and to be drowned in the open sea."*

We see again here the dire warnings directed at anyone who would harm innocents. Jesus' anger seems only to be directed at people who would harm other, less powerful people, not at "sinners."

Other Problematic Theological Concepts

I begin this section with a note about interpretation. My theory of interpretation is that anything that intelligent, dedicated, open-minded commentators disagree about is something that cannot be fully understood by humans. All interpreters believe that their interpretation is correct, but, as a matter of principle, two different interpretations of the same text cannot be both be correct—but they can both be incorrect! Following are a number of concepts that intelligent, dedicated, open-minded commentators disagree about. I'm not claiming that my interpretation of these matters is correct, just that it's consistent with the rest of the text.

A Reasonable Christian Faith

Sin

The traditional Christian term for the fact that there is evil in the world is "sin." The meaning of this term is rather unclear, but a useful place to begin a discussion of what it means is in the theology text, *Christian Theology*, by Millard Erickson. Erickson says:

> Our view of the nature of God influences our understanding of sin. If God is a very high, pure, and exacting being who expects all humans to be as he is, then the slightest deviation from his lofty standard is sin, and man's condition is very serious. If, on the other hand, God is himself rather imperfect, or if he is an indulgent, grandfatherly type of being and perhaps a bit senile so that he is unaware of much that is going on, then man's condition is not so serious. Thus, in a real sense our doctrine of sin will be a reflection of our doctrine of God.[11]

Erickson presents a dichotomy here; either God is "is a very high, pure, and exacting being who expects all humans to be as he is" or God is "rather imperfect, or . . . he is an indulgent, grandfatherly type of being and perhaps a bit senile so that he is unaware of much that is going on." Erickson is correct about the consequences for humans *if* God is one of these ways. But he presents what is called a *false dichotomy*. He only presents us with two options about what God is like, when there are many others. According to Jesus, God is a good father. Good fathers are not "very high, pure, and exacting." They are affirming and loving and supportive. The Jewish religious leaders of Jesus' time were "very high, pure, and exacting." Jesus called them hypocrites. On the other hand, a good father is not an "indulgent, grandfatherly type of being and perhaps a bit senile." In addition to being affirming and loving and supportive, we can take good parents to be active and involved, guiding and directing their children to become good, strong, healthy people. So, Erickson is correct that our view of God will affect (maybe even determine) our view of sin. But since his view of God is limited, so is his view of sin.

---

11. Millard Erickson, *Christian Theology*, 581.

The *Content* of a Reasonable Christian Faith

The term for "sin" mostly used by Jesus in the gospels is "hamartia." The basic meaning of "hamartia" is "to miss the mark." We can take "missing the mark" to refer to a state or an action. We all miss the mark by being weak, ignorant, and insecure in relation to God, just as children are weak, ignorant, and insecure in relation to parents. Is this "bad"? "Bad," in these contexts usually means "shameful." Is being weak, ignorant, and insecure shameful? No. It is just a fact. Children can also "miss the mark" in terms of doing things that are not in line with their parents' ideals or wishes or instructions. Are such actions "bad"? That depends. To use an analogy popular in Christian circles, comparing our faltering attempts to do things to God is like comparing a child who is just learning to walk or to ride a bike to its parents. The child falls down a lot. Is the child bad? No. Are the parents angry and exacting? No. They are excited at each small improvement. They say things like "Don't worry about falling" and "Get up and try again." So, failing because we are small and weak while we are trying to do things, shouldn't make God angry. What about "breaking the rules"? This is the traditional meaning of "sin"—to discuss it I will turn to the biblical story about the origin and consequences of sin.

The Origin of Sin

Adam and Eve

The story of Adam and Eve is well known. Adam and Eve are living in the garden and God comes to visit them and talk to them. He explains that they can eat any of the fruit in the garden, but there is a tree, "the tree of the knowledge of good and evil," that they are not allowed to eat from, or they will "die." The serpent comes, tells them that God is lying, and convinces them to eat the fruit from that tree. They realize they are naked and hide. Then God returns and finds them and determines that they have eaten from the tree. He sends them out of the garden and confers a number of consequences; they will have to work to support themselves, the woman will have lots of pain in childbirth, etc. And, while it is not stated explicitly there, it seems that God will no longer communicate with them directly.

In terms of our image of God as a good parent, this story has good points and bad points. On the good side, God gives pretty clear directions to Adam and Eve, and his command seems to be directed at their well-being (there will be bad consequences if they eat from the tree). God does not seem to be angry in this story; he seems to be just following through with the consequences he has warned about.

On the other hand, there are some problems with this story. One is that God did not spell out the consequences of eating from the tree very completely. He said "you will die." But it is not clear that Adam and Eve would have understood this term (they had never experienced death) and God did not say anything about being sent out of the garden and, worse, did not tell them that he would break off his relationship with them. This doesn't seem fair. Even if God had disclosed all of this, do good parents send their children away and refuse to communicate with them if the children disobey them? Certainly not.

Another problem I have with the story is the tree itself. God created the garden; why did he put this tree in it, then command Adam and Eve to leave it alone? It is often interpreted as a test of Adam and Eve's willingness to obey God. But do good parents set up tests that their children are likely to fail (that they *know* their children will fail, in this case) and then punish and abandon them for failing them? This hardly seems consistent with the notion of a good parent.

I find the story of Adam and Eve unhelpful in understanding God or sin or myself. There are some things that God does not want us to do—that seems clear. But what are those things? The story doesn't seem to answer the question at all—we don't have any trees that we're forbidden from eating from! I find the example of Jesus to be much more instructive than the story with respect to "rules" that we are supposed to obey. The primary rule, according to him, is to love each other.

The *Content* of a Reasonable Christian Faith

There is an interpretation of the story that I find intriguing. It is a well-known psychological fact that children who lose a parent to abandonment, divorce, or death, usually blame themselves for the loss. I think this story can be read as a case of early humans, experiencing a loss of connection with God, blaming themselves for the loss.

Repentance

Conservative Christians place a large focus on repentance, usually connected to feeling shame. I remember many "revival" services in which the leader spoke eagerly about coming forward to an altar and "repenting of your sins." Let's look at what Jesus said about repentance.

> *Matt 3:2 [John speaking] "Repent, for the kingdom of heaven is near."*
>
> *Matt 4:17 From that time Jesus began to preach this message: "Repent, for the kingdom of heaven is near."*
>
> *Matt 11:20 Then Jesus began to criticize openly the cities in which he had done many of his miracles, because they did not repent.*
>
> *Mark 1:4 In the wilderness John the baptizer began preaching a baptism of repentance for the forgiveness of sins.*
>
> *Mark 1:15 Jesus said, "The time is fulfilled and the kingdom of God is near. Repent and believe the gospel!"*
>
> *Mark 6:12 So they [the disciples] went out and preached that all should repent.*
>
> *Luke 3:8 Therefore produce fruit that proves your repentance.*
>
> *Luke 24:46-47 [Jesus] said to them, "Thus it stands written that the Christ would suffer and would rise from the dead on the third day, and repentance for the forgiveness of sins would be proclaimed in his name to all nations, beginning from Jerusalem."*

It is clear that John and Jesus discuss "repentance" in relation to Jesus' message and mission. The question, though, is, what does it mean to "repent"? In the conservative churches in which I was raised, the main concept of "repent" was something like "prostrate yourself before God and feel your immeasurable shame and unworthiness and beg for God to accept you (but God probably won't)." But this is, to me now, an abusive misrepresentation of the meaning of the term. It is a representation fostered by people in power who are seeking to maintain their power by making others submit to them. In short, it is the representation fostered by the Way of Power. In the story of the Prodigal Son, the son wanted to prostrate himself before the father. The father simply didn't allow it. He was just excited about the son's return.

The Greek term translated by "repent" is *metanoeo*. According to Strong's Greek Concordance, *metanoeo* means "I repent, change my mind, change the inner man (particularly with reference to acceptance of the will of God), repent."[12] Nothing is mentioned here about prostration or submission or shame. To repent is to change one's mind. The next question is, what is one changing one's mind about, or what is one changing one's mind *from* and *to*? The conservative answer seems to be that it is ceasing to do a certain set of behaviors, usually drinking, smoking, dancing, and sex. But that is not what Jesus discusses as his mission and message. The core of his message is a change from the Way of Power to the Way of Love. People who have been living the Way of Power could and may be likely to feel remorse and contrition when they realize that they have been living the wrong life, especially if the realization involves the recognition of how they have been disempowering and harming others in their pursuit. But such feelings don't seem necessary. The main act of repentance is the change of how one is living.

Repentance in the passages listed is tied to forgiveness. This makes sense. If people have not changed the way they are living and what they are doing, then forgiveness seems moot. The message of forgiveness is that the past is not determinative of the

12. http://biblehub.com/greek/3340.htm.

The *Content* of a Reasonable Christian Faith

future. The message of repentance is also tied to the discussion of fruit. True repentance involves change; change of lifestyle and change of behavior from the Way of Power to the Way of Love. Again, if my actions and life don't change, it is hard to see in what sense I have "repented."

Belief

The most famous biblical passage about belief is John 3:16:

> *For this is the way God loved the world: He gave his one and only Son, so that everyone who believes in him will not perish but have eternal life.*

I have written a paper about the connection between belief and salvation in the Gospel of John.[13] It mostly has to do with a logical problem in this and other statements by Jesus. Logically, the statement says, "if you believe, then you will have eternal life." This means that everyone who believes (whatever that means) will have eternal life. But it does not mean that everyone who does not believe (whatever that means) does not have eternal life—for that, it must read "if you have eternal life, then you have believed." The status of belief here is a "sufficient" condition, not a "necessary" condition. That means it is open to the possibility that there be other ways to be saved than "belief in Jesus." It follows, for me, that we can be "inclusivists" with regard to salvation—we can believe that people who have never directly met or heard about Jesus can be saved.

Punishment

If we don't do what God wants, or "break the rules", we must continue to look at God as a good father. What do good fathers do when their children disobey? One oft-cited passage from the bible is "spare the rod, spoil the child" (Proverbs 13:24), which is usually

---

13. Daniel Kern, "The Logic of Salvation in the Gospel of John."

used to support beating children. But this is a misinterpretation of the term "rod."

The Shepherd's Rod

The term "rod" in this passage is the same as in the phrase "your rod and staff comfort me," found in Psalm 23. There is an immediate inconsistency between the ideas "use your rod to beat sheep/children" and, from the point of view of a sheep/child, "your rod and your staff comfort me." This inconsistency is validated in an excellent book by Phillip Keller, *A Shepherd Looks at Psalm 23*. He says,

> In caring for his sheep, the good shepherd, the careful manager, will from time to time make a careful examination of each individual sheep. As each animal comes out of the corral and through the gate, it is stopped by the shepherd's outstretched rod. He opens the fleece with the rod; he runs his skillful hands over the body; he feels for any sign of trouble; he examines the sheep with care to see if all is well. This is a most searching process entailing every intimate detail. It is, too, a comfort to the sheep for only in this way can its hidden problems be laid bare before the shepherd.
>
> Finally the shepherd's rod is an instrument of protection both for himself and his sheep when they are in danger. It is used both as a defense and a deterrent against anything that would attack.
>
> The skilled shepherd uses his rod to drive off predators like coyotes, wolves, cougars or stray dogs. Often it is used to beat the brush discouraging snakes and other creatures from disturbing the flock. In extreme cases, such as David recounted to Saul, the psalmist no doubt used his rod to attack the lion and the bear that came to raid his flocks.
>
> The staff has a related use:
>
> The staff is also used for guiding sheep. Again and again I have seen a shepherd use his staff to guide his sheep gently into a new path of through some gate or along dangerous, difficult routes. He does not use it

actually to beat the beast. Rather, the tip of the log slender stick is laid gently against the animals' side and the pressure applied guides the sheep in the way the owner wants it to go. Thus the sheep is reassured of its proper path.[14]

Both the rod and staff, then, are comforts to the sheep. They are used to protect, to guard the well-being of, and to guide the sheep, not to beat or harm them. To spoil children by sparing the rod would be to fail to guard and protect and take care of children, not to refrain from beating them. Similarly, a good father's response to disobedience is direction and support.

Will God punish certain people eternally in hell? Well, we can ask, would a good father subject his children to eternal torture, whatever they said or did? The story of the prodigal son gives us the answer—no. And, as we have seen, God must be committed to human happiness. To subject someone to eternal torture is not consistent with being committed to their happiness. The question of what would happen to people who don't want to be with God is an interesting question; I will deal with it later.

Obedience

The Way of Power relies heavily on obedience, because obedience shows submission and control, which are the main stock of power. By this point, we should expect a different approach to obedience by Jesus. The discussion of obedience in the section above about fruit shows this different approach. Jesus obeys his father and asks that his followers obey him. But "obey" here really just means "follow" or "do as Jesus does." It is hard to imagine saying "I follow Jesus, but I don't obey him," or "I follow Jesus, but I don't do what he did." And what does Jesus do and command? He loves people, acting sacrificially to promote their good.

---

14. Phillip Keller, *A Shepherd Looks at Psalm 23*, 116.

Submission

The Way of Power relies heavily on submission, because submission reveals and solidifies hierarchy and control. Jesus clearly submitted himself to God's plans. He famously prays, before he is crucified, "My father, if possible, let this cup pass from me! Yet not what I will, but what you will." Jesus was carrying out a plan of and for his Father. But the plan was not to accumulate power for the father, it was to love people by dying for them. If God has a particular plan for you or me, I assume God will let us know (although the world is filled with people who claim they are following God's plan, when clearly they aren't!). Since we are involved in the work of loving people as commanded by Jesus, to that extent, we should submit to Jesus. But, again, it's not an expression of power; it's an expression of love.

Salvation

To begin, we can review some of the places where the term "saved" is used in the Gospels.

> Matt 1:21 *She will give birth to a son and you will name him Jesus, because he will save his people from their sins."*
>
> Matt 9:21 *For she kept saying to herself, "If only I touch his cloak, I will be healed."*
>
> Matt 10:22 *(also Mark 13:13 and Matt 24:13) The one who endures to the end will be saved.*
>
> Mark 16:16 *The one who believes and is baptized will be saved.*
>
> Luke 8:50 *(regarding a girl who had died) Do not fear, only believe, and she will be healed.*
>
> John 10:9 *I am the door; anyone who enters by me will be saved.*

Based on the texts above, the term "saved" is used in many places with many meanings in the Gospels. Its root meaning is, "to save, to keep safe and sound, to rescue from danger or destruction."[15] This is consistent with Jesus' self-proclamation of being here to set prisoners free. What are we "saved" from? One possibility is hell, which I will discuss shortly. Another possibility is that we are set free from the Way of Power and able to live with the Way of Love.

Hopeful Inclusivism

There are other references to salvation in the Gospels:

> Matt 7:21-23 "Not everyone who says to me, 'Lord, Lord,' will enter into the kingdom of heaven—only the one who does the will of my Father in heaven. On that day, many will say to me, 'Lord, Lord, didn't we prophesy in your name, and in your name cast out demons and do many powerful deeds?' Then I will declare to them, 'I never knew you. Go away from me, you lawbreakers!'
>
> John 12:32 And I, when I am lifted up from the earth, will draw all people to myself.

In the first text, Jesus is talking about who will be "saved," in terms of entering the kingdom of heaven. Here he mentions doing lots of things "in the name of Jesus." Jesus is clear that this is not sufficient for entering the kingdom of heaven. Although he doesn't state exactly what is required here, clearly doing deeds "in the name of Jesus" is not sufficient. In the second text Jesus makes a universal claim, that he will draw all people to himself. This claim makes it sound like everyone will be saved! I will discuss this idea more in the next section, hell.

Hell

The subject of Hell is a notoriously difficult and problematic subject. Jesus uses troubling phrases regarding the fate of certain people. He uses a number of terms for this idea. One is "Gehenna."

---

15. https://biblehub.com/greek/4982.htm.

"Gehenna" is "a Greek transliteration of the Hebrew words ge hinnom ("Valley of Hinnom"). This was the valley along the south side of Jerusalem. In [Old Testament] times it was used for human sacrifices to the pagan god Molech, and it came to be used as a place where human excrement and rubbish were disposed of and burned. In the intertestamental period, it came to be used symbolically as the place of divine punishment."[16] The important thing here is that "Gehenna" is being used symbolically, which leaves it open as to what the correct interpretation is.

Perhaps the best thing to do is to look at some of the uses of "hell" by Jesus. One of the most instructive things is to whom he refers as being in danger of hell. The first I've cited before:

> *Matt 25:31–45* "When the Son of Man comes in his glory and all the angels with him, then he will sit on his glorious throne. All the nations will be assembled before him, and he will separate people one from another like a shepherd separates the sheep from the goats. He will put the sheep on his right and the goats on his left. Then the king will say to those on his right, 'Come, you who are blessed by my Father, inherit the kingdom prepared for you from the foundation of the world. For I was hungry and you gave me food, I was thirsty and you gave me something to drink, I was a stranger and you invited me in, I was naked and you gave me clothing, I was sick and you took care of me, I was in prison and you visited me.' Then the righteous will answer him, 'Lord, when did we see you hungry and feed you, or thirsty and give you something to drink? When did we see you a stranger and invite you in, or naked and clothe you? When did we see you sick or in prison and visit you?' And the king will answer them, 'I tell you the truth, just as you did it for one of the least of these brothers or sisters of mine, you did it for me.'
>
> "Then he will say to those on his left, 'Depart from me, you accursed, into the eternal fire that has been prepared for the devil and his angels! For I was hungry and you gave me nothing to eat, I was thirsty and you gave me nothing to drink. I was a stranger and you did not receive me as a

---

16. Netbible.org, note to Matt 5:22.

The *Content* of a Reasonable Christian Faith

> guest, naked and you did not clothe me, sick and in prison and you did not visit me.' Then they too will answer, 'Lord, when did we see you hungry or thirsty or a stranger or naked or sick or in prison, and did not give you whatever you needed?' Then he will answer them, 'I tell you the truth, just as you did not do it for one of the least of these, you did not do it for me.' And these will depart into eternal punishment, but the righteous into eternal life."

This is a pretty sobering description of the fate of certain people. There are a couple of interesting things about it, though. One is that "eternal fire" has not been prepared for people at all, but for "the devil and his angels." Another is who is in danger of going to this place. It says nothing about belief, but only presents a list of things that could be summarized as "helping others." It doesn't specify how much helping is required, so it is a rather ambiguous criterion.

> Matt 5:22 But I say to you that anyone who is angry with a brother will be subjected to judgment. And whoever insults a brother will be brought before the council, and whoever says 'Fool' will be sent to fiery hell.

Who is in danger here? This time it's anyone who is angry or calls someone a "fool."

> Matt 23:33 [to Pharisees] You snakes, you offspring of vipers! How will you escape being condemned to hell?

The notable thing here again is to whom Jesus is speaking. Here, it's the Pharisees—the religious leaders of the time!

> Luke 16:19-25 "There was a rich man who dressed in purple and fine linen and who feasted sumptuously every day. But at his gate lay a poor man named Lazarus whose body was covered with sores, who longed to eat what fell from the rich man's table. In addition, the dogs came and licked his sores.
>
> "Now the poor man died and was carried by the angels to Abraham's side. The rich man also died and was buried. And in hell, as he was in torment, he looked up and saw Abraham far off with Lazarus at his side. So he

> called out, 'Father Abraham, have mercy on me, and send Lazarus to dip the tip of his finger in water and cool my tongue, because I am in anguish in this fire.' But Abraham said, 'Child, remember that in your lifetime you received your good things and Lazarus likewise bad things, but now he is comforted here and you are in anguish.'"

Once again, the person in danger here is not who is expected. In this case there is a clear distinction between rich and poor—the implication is that rich people go to hell and poor people go to heaven.

> Matt 10:28 Do not be afraid of those who kill the body but cannot kill the soul. Instead, fear the one who is able to destroy both soul and body in hell.

The interesting thing about this passage is the fate of those in hell. To destroy both body and soul sounds like one is totally annihilated and ceases to exist.

What can we make of all these references to hell? The word is used symbolically, inconsistently, and doesn't seem to be directed at the people that conservative Christians usually think are in danger. My conclusion is that there is not enough concrete evidence to draw any concrete conclusions.

Is it reasonable to believe that God will punish humans forever in hell? I think it's not, for several reasons. One is that, as I've said, God must be committed to human happiness, or God is not worthy of our worship (and we are not able to worship God, even if we fear God). Another is the fact that God is a good father—it seems inconsistent that a good father would condemn any of his children to eternal torment. The father of the prodigal son never gave up hoping that his son would return. The possible exception to this is that certain people may not (ever) choose to be with God. It's hard to know what God would do with people who don't desire to be with him. At least, it seems that he would forever hope for their return . . .

The *Content* of a Reasonable Christian Faith

Heaven

Heaven is popularly presented as a world with angels floating around playing harps, or, more biblically, a city with streets of gold.[17] Jesus never uses such terms. In one place he discusses "places to stay" in his father's house.[18] In the earlier passage about the rich man and poor man in heaven and hell, Jesus says that the poor man "was carried by the angels to Abraham's side," which is not very instructive. In a number of parables and other places in the Bible, there is a discussion of a wedding banquet.

> *Isa 25:6-8 The Lord who commands armies will hold a banquet for all the nations on this mountain.*
> *At this banquet there will be plenty of meat and aged wine—tender meat and choicest wine.*
> *On this mountain he will swallow up*
> *the shroud that is over all the peoples,*
> *the woven covering that is over all the nations;*
> *he will swallow up death permanently.*
> *The sovereign Lord will wipe away the tears from every face,*
> *and remove his people's disgrace from all the earth.*
> *Indeed, the Lord has announced it!*

This is a very interesting passage. Note that the prediction here says nothing about angels or clouds or trumpets; it just says that God will provide a banquet (note, for "all the nations" and "all the peoples"), and will wipe away the tears from every face. Another popular conception of heaven is that God will explain everything to us. But here, God doesn't explain anything; the people just say "let's celebrate." I will discuss this more in the *Challenges* section of this book.

---

17. The "streets of gold" reference comes from the book of the Revelation, which, according to my theory that anything that intelligent people disagree about is not understood, is not understood.

18. John 14:2, my translation.

Conclusion

To summarize this section; Jesus portrays God as a good father. As a preliminary characterization, a good father is one who gives his children freedom, who waits patiently for them if they are gone, forgives them when they make mistakes, who does not act out of anger or vindictiveness or desire for punishment, who gives them what they (really) need, and who loves them and is delighted by them. The four eye-witness accounts of Jesus' life in the Bible are called the "gospels." "Gospel" means "good news"—remember the angels' words to the shepherds at Christmas: "we bring you good news ("gospel") of great joy to all people." The news of an angry, punishing, vindictive God is not good news—but the news of the God as a good father that Jesus introduces us to is really good news!

JESUS AND THE REST OF THE BIBLE

How does what I am saying relate to the rest of the bible? What about all of the passages that say that God is angry and punishing, like Noah's Flood? A common principle of biblical interpretation is that we must interpret what is unclear in light of what is clear.[19] We are taking Jesus to be the clearest presentation of who God is and what God wants. Take "God is a good father" and "God is angry, vindictive, and judgmental." I claim that these statements are inconsistent. Remember from our earlier discussion that if two statements are inconsistent, it is impossible for them both to be true, and it is irrational to assert that they are both true. Jesus showed us what "good father" means, and his portrayal consciously excludes angry, vindictive, judgementalism, because those were the expected aspects of fatherhood at his time (and ours, too, for that matter). We must choose between these definitions. How do we

---

19. This principle is usually attributed to Augustine. For instance, he says in *On Christian Doctrine*, "investigate the obscure passages, and in doing so draw examples from the plainer expressions to throw light upon the more obscure." *On Christian Doctrine*, Book 2, Chapter 9, Paragraph 14.

The *Content* of a Reasonable Christian Faith

choose? Taoism and Augustine[20] provide an answer. When individuals experience transcendent reality, they have to use the signs, concepts, or words available to them to interpret the experience. The writers of the Old Testament (and New Testament) lived in a patriarchal world. In that world, rulers were kings and fathers who ruled by assertion of power. Those rulers were angry, vindictive, judgmental rulers, because their power was insecure, and they had to protect it aggressively. So if they experienced a transcendent reality that was powerful, they would interpret that power as insecure patriarchal power. Jesus shows his transcendence by being able to take the cultural picture of fatherhood and redefine it in the face of the expectations of the people around him.

The angry, punishing father is not even the only picture of God we find in the Old Testament. In Exodus 34:6–7, God mentions both sides of his Old Testament character:

> *The Lord passed by before [Moses] and proclaimed: "The Lord, the Lord, the compassionate and gracious God, slow to anger, and abounding in loyal love and faithfulness, keeping loyal love for thousands, forgiving iniquity and transgression and sin. But he by no means leaves the guilty unpunished, responding to the transgression of fathers by dealing with children and children's children, to the third and fourth generation."*

In Luke 4:18–19, when Jesus announces his ministry, he quotes from Isaiah:

> *The Spirit of the Lord is upon me,*
> *because he has anointed me to proclaim good news to the poor.*
> *He has sent me to proclaim release to the captives*
> *and the regaining of sight to the blind,*
> *to set free those who are oppressed,*
> *to proclaim the year of the Lord's favor.*[21]

---

20. In "What a Thing Is, and What A Sign," Augustine explains that we have to use the signs available to us to name things. *On Christian Doctrine*, Book 1, Chapter 2.

21. Quoting from Isa 61:1–2.

There are also a number of passages in which God says he desires mercy and justice, rather than sacrifices.[22]

The Old Testament view of God is inconsistent. When we read a passage that says or seems to say that God is angry, vindictive and judgmental (and that he wants us to be that way), we can interpret it as a misinterpretation of what was going on. We must interpret such passages in light of what it means to be a good father, as shown to us by Jesus.

I don't feel obligated to hold that inconsistent claims are all true; in fact, I feel rationally obligated *not* to try to hold them as true. I have a basis for making distinctions; the life and words of Jesus. So I believe that I am being both biblical and rational to use Jesus' image of the good father recorded in the gospel accounts as my primary and overriding image of who and what God is, even if I have to reinterpret other claims from the Bible when they contradict this image.

---

22. For instance, Psa 51:17, Prov 21:3, Isa 1:11, and Mic 6:8.

Part 3

Applications of a Reasonable Christian Faith

THE LGBTQIA+ COMMUNITY

How CHRISTIANS ARE TO be with respect to the LGBTQIA+ community is one of the main theological issues of our time. How would a reasonable Christian understand their position? I hope to present a consistent, reasonable position that Christians can hold.

The words of Jesus that are used most often in relation to the question of LGBTQIA+ persons and relationships are these;

> Matt 19:3-9 *Then some Pharisees came to him in order to test him. They asked, "Is it lawful to divorce a wife for any cause?" He answered, "Have you not read that from the beginning the Creator made them male and female, and said, 'For this reason a man will leave his father and mother and will be united with his wife, and the two will become one flesh'? So they are no longer two, but one flesh. Therefore, what God has joined together, let no one separate." They said to him, "Why then did Moses command us to give a certificate of dismissal and to divorce her?" Jesus said to them, "Moses permitted you to divorce your wives because of your hard hearts, but from the beginning it was not this way. Now I say to you that whoever divorces his*

wife, except for immorality, and marries another commits adultery."

To begin, the Pharisees were not asking Jesus for theological or moral clarification; they were trying to trap Jesus into saying something they could use against him. Jesus usually responded to these attempts by the Pharisees by posing a puzzle in return—he almost never answered the Pharisees directly. So Jesus' word here, to begin with, must be interpreted carefully.

Let us consider the interpretation that Jesus is alerting us to an ideal instituted by God. We might express it as "God's ideal for human relationships is for one man to be married to one woman for life." But it's not entirely clear what this means. If this is God's ideal for *all* human relationships, wouldn't it imply that *everyone* should be married? Wouldn't that imply that being single is morally wrong? And is there a certain age by which everyone must be married? What is it? What about a person who is that age but can't find anyone to marry? And would it require that widows and widowers remarry? How soon after the death of the previous spouse?

If Jesus' quote is to be taken as setting an absolute standard, what does it make of the polygamous marriages of the Old Testament? If Old Testament Hebrews could be accepted by God while breaking this marriage command, then other forms of marriage could be accepted by God.

God allowed marriages to be separated by divorce. That's an important point, and one that has been used to justify many Christian remarriages, which seems to go against Jesus' literal words in the same passage. Remarriage would go against God's original ideal for humans. And then there seems to be a conflict for the divorced person between a demand to be married and a demand not to be remarried.

I made a point earlier about good parents and happiness. Parents have ideals for their children. But if those ideals are too specific and are imposed on their children without regard for the uniqueness and individuality of the child, they become overbearing and stilting. One of the primary characteristics of good parents is that they foster the individuality of their children and allow their children to grow into their unique selves. I would argue that the only goal that good parents should have for their children is that their children be happy. The only direct criterion applied by Jesus to happiness is to love. Part of the model of good parenting that I'm advocating is that good parents provide freedom for children to develop into what they are (limited by the requirement to love), not what parents want them to be. Is it going too far to believe that this must be how God deals with us? The Way of Power says God knows everything, has strict guidelines for us to follow, and demands that we not stray from the specific path determined by God, or else anger and punishment will ensue. But that is precisely the way I am challenging, and I am arguing that Jesus challenges the Way of Power, with the Way of Love.

Judgment and Fruit

If we are trying to decide how to interpret lifestyles or behaviors of other members of our communities, I'd like to look at three passages that seem to address such situations. The first is about judgment:

> Matt 7:1-5 "Do not judge so that you will not be judged. For by the standard you judge you will be judged, and the measure you use will be the measure you receive. Why do you see the speck in your brother's eye, but fail to see the beam of wood in your own? Or how can you say to your brother, 'Let me remove the speck from your eye,' while there is a beam in your own? You hypocrite! First remove the beam from your own eye, and then you can see clearly to remove the speck from your brother's eye.

In this strong, but somewhat comical passage, Jesus is very clear about what God thinks of people judging other people's lives and actions: we will be judged by God by the same criteria that we use to judge others. That, more than anything else Jesus said, frightens me! It makes me want to be very affirming and accepting in all of my evaluations of others.

The second is about fruit:

> Matt 7:15-20 *"Watch out for false prophets, who come to you in sheep's clothing but inwardly are voracious wolves. You will recognize them by their fruit. Grapes are not gathered from thorns or figs from thistles, are they? In the same way, every good tree bears good fruit, but the bad tree bears bad fruit. A good tree is not able to bear bad fruit, nor a bad tree to bear good fruit. Every tree that does not bear good fruit is cut down and thrown into the fire. So then, you will recognize them by their fruit.*

This passage is again quite practical. If there are people in our communities whose lifestyles or behaviors we question, there is a practical criterion; look at the person's fruit. The "fruit" I have been discussing is simple: love. Remember, Paul, in his letter to the Galatians, says (5:22-23), "But the fruit of the Spirit is love, joy, peace, patience, kindness, goodness, faithfulness, gentleness, and self-control. Against such things there is no law." The question then, regarding LGTBQIA+ persons (as it is for all persons), is, are they displaying these fruit? There seems to be no more problem for LGTBQIA+ persons than for any other person to display these qualities. And combining this passage with the earlier one, if people want to evaluate others with these criteria, they should be sure that they are embodying them themselves—and if they are, they will be loving, joyful, peaceful, patient, kind, good, and faithful in their analysis of others.

One other passage may be instructive in this light:

> Matt 13:24-30 *[Jesus] presented them with another parable: "The kingdom of heaven is like a person who sowed good seed in his field. But while everyone was sleeping, an enemy came and sowed weeds among the wheat and went away. When the plants sprouted and bore grain, then the weeds also appeared. So the slaves of the owner came and said to him, 'Sir, didn't you sow good seed in your field? Then where did the weeds come from?' He said, 'An enemy has done this.' So the slaves replied, 'Do you want us to go and gather them?' But he said, 'No, since in gathering the weeds you may uproot the wheat with them. Let both grow together until the harvest. At harvest time I will tell the*

Applications of a Reasonable Christian Faith

reapers, "First collect the weeds and tie them in bundles to be burned, but then gather the wheat into my barn.""

This is a more complex criterion. Here's how I read it. Suppose there are people in a community whose behavior or lifestyle are different than our own. Jesus seems to be saying we shouldn't "gather" or "uproot" them (which I take to mean attacking them or trying to get rid of them), because we might "uproot" the "wheat" with them. The idea, I think, is that if we show the kind of judgmentalism involved in uprooting people from our communities because they look or act different than us, then we might offend and chase away good, innocent people as well. Does this mean we should allow dangerous people to remain among our groups? I think there is a reasonable balance here, but I also think that Jesus' warnings about judgment are among the strongest things he said, and we should always give people as much benefit of the doubt as we can. Given that we have the "fruit" criterion, that could serve as a useful criterion for when to interpret people who appear different in a church setting.

Happiness

Good parents want their children to be happy. But parents know a lot more about human nature and happiness than children do. So the fact that children believe that something will make them happy is not in itself a good reason for the parent to give it to them. We often refuse to give our children things that they ask for, because we want them to be happy. So the fact that people believe that some activity or relationship will make them happy is not necessarily a good argument that it will make them happy in the long run (and this is true for everyone). But, two points. First: children grow up and should follow their own paths, whatever the parents think about their happiness. Second, there is no reason to believe (and no data to support) that LGBTQIA+ people aren't as happy as anyone else.

There is another argument related to happiness that is sometimes offered; that God will punish LGBTQIA+ people in the afterlife, which will make them unhappy, so that whatever happiness they experience in this life, it will be outweighed by the unhappiness they will experience later. But this argument is fundamentally at odds with the image of God that I am endorsing here, and I would argue that no person should take this as a possibility, as I argued in my discussion of Hell.

So what would Jesus say to LGBTQIA+ people? The same thing as he said to the woman at the well who was living, unmarried, with a man—"I offer you living water, with no conditions attached."

Part 4

Challenges to a Reasonable Christian Faith

Although I am arguing that it is possible to hold a reasonable Christian faith, I do not find it easy. Here I take up what I find to be the major challenges to a reasonable Christian faith.

THE ABSENCE OF GOD

I find the issue of the God's absence to be the most troubling issue for my own faith (perhaps because I have not experienced extreme suffering). It seems like a necessary aspect of being a good parent that you are present with and to your children. But God is not here.

I have no good resolution to this problem. It doesn't make sense to me. One traditional answer is that God doesn't want to overwhelm people; God wants people who will respond to him in faith. This doesn't seem right to me—God could have limited his presence on earth without removing it entirely. Another response is that God did come into the world in Eden and in Jesus. But I find this explanation unsatisfactory as well. It seems like good parents wouldn't go away and leave their children for long periods of time with no communication. Good parents want to be with their children, interacting and relating.

Another unsatisfactory answer is that this world is some sort of testing ground, and the people who "pass" the test without God's presence will be rewarded. The story of the Garden of Eden is supposed to describe this answer to the question. Adam and Eve had a test to pass; they failed it. So God sent them out of the garden and was with them no longer. But this specific answer and this general answer don't work for me. Adam and Eve failed the test in God's presence! As I mentioned in an earlier discussion, the Adam and Eve story reminds me of the fact that children whose parents have left them always blame themselves for the loss, when is not their fault at all.

WHY THE WORLD IS THE WAY IT IS

In my more pessimistic moments, the world seems to me like a very bad joke or a maze that we have been stuck in for the amusement of some cosmic sadist or inept creator, not the creation of a benevolent, loving, powerful parent. David Hume poses this problem in his work, *Dialogues Concerning Natural Religion*. He wrote,

> It must, I think, be allowed, that if a very limited intelligence, whom we shall suppose utterly unacquainted with the universe, were assured, that it were the production of a very good, wise, and powerful Being, however finite, he would, from his conjectures, form beforehand a different notion of it from what we find it to be by experience; nor would he ever imagine, merely from these attributes of the cause [God], of which he is informed, that the effect [the world] could be so full of vice and misery and disorder, as it appears in this life. . .
>
> Did I show you a house or palace, where there was not one apartment convenient or agreeable; where the windows, doors, fires, passages, stairs, and the whole economy of the building, were the source of noise, confusion, fatigue, darkness, and the extremes of heat and cold; you would certainly blame the contrivance, without any further examination. The architect would in vain display his subtlety, and prove to you, that if this door or

that window were altered, greater ills would ensue. What he says may be strictly true: The alteration of one particular, while the other parts of the building remain, may only augment the inconveniences. But still you would assert in general, that, if the architect had had skill and good intentions, he might have formed such a plan of the whole, and might have adjusted the parts in such a manner, as would have remedied all or most of these inconveniences. His ignorance, or even your own ignorance of such a plan, will never convince you of the impossibility of it. If you find any inconveniences and deformities in the building, you will always, without entering into any detail, condemn the architect.[1]

The gist of the argument here is, if God is so loving, powerful and intelligent, why is the world so poorly made? Why are people so weak? Why do people make so many bad choices? Why are there so many natural disasters (the question of pain and suffering will be dealt with next)? If we saw a building that was very poorly made, we would infer that the builder was limited in power, intelligence, willingness to make a good structure, or all three. On the other side, if we imagined a world made by a loving, powerful and intelligent being, we would imagine a world that worked better than this one does.

The "this is a test" answer is also proposed for this problem. My response is the same here. Would good parents put their children in a test with such insuperable odds against them (natural disaster, suffering, and death) and such dire consequences (God's absence, death, hell)? I can't imagine doing that to my children.

PAIN AND SUFFERING

It is with great trepidation that I broach the problem of pain and suffering. For anyone that has endured extreme pain and suffering, any attempt by another person to resolve the deep, soul-wracking emotions that it creates must sound hollow and offensive. So I will

1. Hume, *Dialogues Concerning Natural Religion*, Part 11.

not try to "solve" or "resolve" the problem. I have no resolution for or explanation of pain and suffering, and no answer to the question of why a God whom I am portraying as a good parent would allow it (at least at the level that we experience it).

The most powerful expression of the theological problem of pain and suffering that I have seen was written by Fyodor Dostoevsky in *The Brothers Karamazov*. In this passage, Ivan Karamazov is speaking to his brother Fyodor, who is studying to become a priest. This passage is quite long, but it presents the problem as an insurmountable problem with such passion that it is worth reading.

> Ivan was silent for a moment; his face suddenly became very sad.
>
> "Listen to me: I took children only so as to make it more obvious. About all the other human tears that have soaked the whole earth through from crust to core, I don't say a word, I've purposely narrowed down my theme. I am a bedbug, and I confess in all humility that I can understand nothing of why it's all arranged as it is. So people themselves are to blame: they were given paradise, they wanted freedom, and stole fire from heaven, knowing that they would become unhappy—so why pity them? Oh, with my pathetic, earthly, Euclidean mind, I know only there is suffering, that none are to blame, that all things follow simply and directly one from another, that everything flows and finds its level—but that is all just Euclidean gibberish, of course I know that, and of course I cannot consent to live by it! What do I care that none are to blame and that I know it—I need retribution, otherwise I will destroy myself. And retribution not somewhere and sometime in infinity, but here and now, on earth, so that I see it myself. I have believed, and I want to see for myself, and if I am dead by that time, let them resurrect me, because it will be too unfair if it all takes place without me.
>
> Is it possible that I've suffered so that I, together with my evil deeds and sufferings, should be manure for someone's future harmony? I want to see with my own eyes the hind lie down with the lion, and the murdered

man rise up and embrace his murderer. I want to be there when everyone suddenly finds out what it was all for. All religions in the world are based on this desire, and I am a believer. But then there are the children, and what am I going to do with them? That is the question I cannot resolve. For the hundredth time I repeat: there are hosts of questions, but I've taken only the children, because here what I need to say is irrefutably clear. Listen: if everyone must suffer, in order to buy eternal harmony with their suffering, pray tell me what have children got to do with it? It's quite incomprehensible why they should have to suffer, and why they should buy harmony with their suffering. Why do they get thrown on the pile, to manure someone's future with themselves? I understand solidarity in sin among men; solidarity in retribution I also understand; but what solidarity in sin do little children have? And if it is really true that they, too, are in solidarity with their fathers in all the fathers' evildoings, that truth certainly is not of this world and is incomprehensible to me.

Some joker will say, perhaps, that in any case the child will grow up and have time enough to sin, but there is this boy who didn't grow up but was torn apart by dogs at the age of eight. Oh, Alyosha, I'm not blaspheming! I do understand how the universe will tremble when all in heaven and under the earth merge in one voice of praise, and all that lives and has ever lived cries out: 'Just art thou, O Lord, for thy ways are revealed!' Oh, yes, when the mother and the torturer whose hounds tore her son to pieces embrace each other and all three cry out with tears: 'Just art thou, O Lord,' then of course the crown of knowledge will have come and everything will be explained. But there is the hitch: that is what I cannot accept. And while I am on earth I hasten to take my own measures. You see, Alyosha, it may well be that if I live until that moment, or rise again in order to see it, I myself will perhaps cry out with all the rest, looking at the mother embracing her child's tormentor: 'Just art thou, O Lord!' But I do not want to cry out with them. While there is still time, I hasten to defend myself against it, and therefore I absolutely renounce all higher harmony. It is not worth one little tear of even that one tormented child who beat her chest with her little fist and prayed to 'dear God' in a stinking outhouse with her unredeemed tears! Not worth it, because her tears remain unredeemed. They must be redeemed, otherwise there can be no harmony.

But how, how will you redeem them? Is it possible? Can they be redeemed by being avenged? But what do I care if they are avenged, what do I care if the tormentors are in hell, what can hell set right here, if these ones have already been tormented? And where is the harmony, if there is hell? I want to forgive, and I want to embrace, I don't want more suffering. I assert beforehand that the whole of truth is not worth such a price. I do not, finally, want the mother to embrace the tormentor who let his dogs tear her son to pieces! She dare not forgive him! Let her forgive him for herself, if she wants to, let her forgive the tormentor her immeasurable maternal suffering; but she has no right to forgive the suffering of her child who was torn to pieces, she dare not forgive the tormentor even if the child himself were to forgive him! And if that is so, if they dare not forgive, then where is the harmony? Is there in the whole world a being who could and would have the right to forgive? I don't want harmony, for love of mankind I don't want it. I want to remain with unrequited suffering. I'd rather remain with my unrequited suffering and my own unquenched indignation, *even if I am wrong*. Besides, they have put too high a price on harmony; we can't afford to pay so much for admission. And therefore I hasten to return my ticket. And it is my duty, if only as an honest man, to return it as far ahead of time as possible. Which is what I am doing. It's not that I don't accept God, Alyosha, I just most respectfully return him the ticket."[2]

Ivan notes that none of the "resolutions" of pain and suffering work. Suffering can't be "atoned for" in the sense of being taken away or forgotten. Punishing wrongdoers can't take suffering away. Ivan decides to "give back the ticket" in response to this fact. Having my own children, I deeply feel Ivan's critique. What if my

2. Dostoevsky, *The Brothers Karamazov*, 259.

Challenges to a Reasonable Christian Faith

children were tortured? Here is another deep expression of this sentiment, written by Elie Wiesel:

> Let us try to imagine what goes on in his mind as his eyes watch rings of black smoke unfurl in the sky, smoke that emanates from the furnaces into which his little sister and his mother had been thrown after thousands of other victims:
>
> Never shall I forget that night, the first night in camp, that turned my life into one long night seven times sealed.
>
> Never shall I forget that smoke.
>
> Never shall I forget the small faces of the children whose bodies I saw transformed into smoke under a silent sky.
>
> Never shall I forget those flames that consumed my faith forever.
>
> Never shall I forget the nocturnal silence that deprived me for all eternity of the desire to live.
>
> Never shall I forget those moments that murdered my God and my soul and turned my dreams to ashes.
>
> Never shall I forget those things, even were I condemned to live as long as God Himself.
>
> Never.[3]

There is really no response to such sentiments. It is not clear that Christianity teaches that suffering is, to use Ivan's term, "atoned for." "Atonement" is a theological term coined in the 16th century to refer to what happened when Jesus died on the cross and rose again.[4] I have no problem saying that I don't understand why Jesus died and rose—theologians have been debating the meaning of Jesus' death and resurrection since they happened, which, to me, means that no one understands what they mean. Does the fact that Jesus suffered and died fix the problem of pain and suffering?

---

3. Wiesel, *Night*, 22.

4. "Atonement" means "Reparation, in Christian belief the reconciliation of God and mankind through Jesus Christ. The word comes (in the early 16th century, denoting unity or reconciliation, especially between God and man), from 'at one' + the suffix '-ment'." https://www.oxfordreference.com/view/10.1093/oi/authority.20110803095432363.

Ivan's and Wiesel's points seem to be, rightly, that it doesn't. What it does show is that God and Jesus are willing to suffer along with us and they understand suffering. That may be (and, I believe, is) all that can be said.

The bible doesn't "explain" suffering. Even in Job, the most direct addressing of suffering in the Bible, God doesn't explain himself. Here's what God says to Job:

> Job 40:6–14 Then the Lord answered Job from the whirlwind:
> "Get ready for a difficult task like a man.
> I will question you, and you will inform me.
> Would you indeed annul my justice?
> Would you declare me guilty so that you might be right?
> Do you have an arm as powerful as God's,
> and can you thunder with a voice like his?
> Adorn yourself, then, with majesty and excellency,
> and clothe yourself with glory and honor.
> Scatter abroad the abundance of your anger.
> Look at every proud man and bring him low.
> Look at every proud man and abase him;
> crush the wicked on the spot.
> Hide them in the dust together;
> imprison them in the grave.
> Then I myself will acknowledge to you
> that your own right hand can save you."

This is strong language. My point is just that God doesn't necessarily justify suffering. God does describe the ultimate end of things, though. As I discussed in my discussion of heaven, it is that one day we will encounter a reality that is so great that it can make people, even those who have endured extreme pain and suffering, not forget their suffering, but somehow move past it. The New Testament writer Paul uses the expression that death is "swallowed up" by this reality.[5]

Ivan understands this "resolution" and he rejects it. He talks about the parents of children who have suffered and the children and the perpetrators all facing each other and forgiving each other. He says, that even if they do forgive each other, "I would rather

---

5. 1 Cor 15:54; citing Isa 25:8.

Challenges to a Reasonable Christian Faith

be left with the unavenged suffering. I would rather remain with my unavenged suffering and unsatisfied indignation, even if I were wrong." Ivan seems to be saying that even if the people who have suffered embrace the new reality, he won't. He says he will "protect" himself so that even if he feels like embracing the new reality, he will be able to stop himself.

It is possible that Ivan goes too far in his response. The people who have suffered (of which I am not one, I admit) would be the test case for the acceptability of this new reality. The implication from the Isaiah passage cited in my discussion of Heaven is that people who have suffered will be able to accept and embrace it. If that is the case, then what more could be required? Ivan says that what he doesn't want to say is "You are just." But the biblical picture is not that God justifies himself in the end, just that he "wipes the tears" from everyone's eyes.

I try to imagine Ivan on that day. I imagine him at a door, with the sounds of a raucous feast on the other side, and God standing by the door, welcoming him in. Ivan says, "You have to justify suffering first." God says "I can't explain or justify suffering in a way that is accessible to you. But look around; many people who have suffered terribly are at the table, feasting and celebrating. Please come in and join us. Suffering is over; it's a new world." We now return to the relationship between faith and reason. It seems possible, and consistent with biblical theology, that Ivan could refuse the invitation. But would Ivan be being reasonable to refuse?

I can sympathize with someone who has experienced extreme suffering feeling that nothing could "atone" for their suffering. But again, the picture here is not one of atonement or justification or explanation. It's a picture of one reality (containing terrible and unexplained suffering) ending, and another reality, not containing suffering (although it seems to include the memory of suffering), taking its place. There seems to be just a choice of whether to enter the new reality or not. Maybe Ivan would have grounds for not accepting this reality, but there certainly seem to be reasonable grounds for accepting it. What if people didn't accept it? This again raises the question of what if people don't want to be with God? I assume God wouldn't force them to be in his presence; I suspect God would wait patiently (forever) for them to change their mind.

Conclusion

I HOPE I HAVE made a convincing case that it is reasonable to believe that there is a God who created the world and us, that Jesus is the best representation we have of that God and what that God is like, and that God is able to be loved and worshiped by us. I haven't tried to "prove" anything, but to present a case that it is reasonable to believe these things. Some things, like miracles, go beyond what human reason would expect, but they don't go against human reason.

The New Atheists are correct that much hatred has been exhibited by, and much pain and suffering have been caused by, supposed followers of Jesus and God. However, given the natures of Jesus and God as I have presented them here, the people that have exhibited and caused such things in Jesus' name are not followers of Jesus or the God he represents. I will end with Jesus' warning;

> Matt 7:20 "So then, you will recognize them by their fruit. Not everyone who says to me, 'Lord, Lord,' will enter into the kingdom of heaven—only the one who does the will of my Father in heaven."

Bibliography

Aquinas, St. Thomas. *Summa Theologia.* Translated by Fathers of the English Dominican Province. Second and Revised Edition. Notre Dame: Ave Maria, 1920.
Aristotle. *Metaphysics.* Translated by W. D. Ross. Oxford: Clarendon, 1952.
———. *Nichomachean Ethics.* Translated by W. D. Ross. Oxford: Clarendon, 1952.
———. *Physics.* Translated by W. D. Ross. Oxford: Clarendon, 1952.
———. *Rhetoric.* Translated by J. H. Freese. Cambridge: Harvard University Press, 1929. http://www.perseus.tufts.edu/hopper/text?doc=Perseus%3Atext%3A1999.01.0060%3Abook%3D1%3Achapter%3D10%3Asection%3D8.
Auslander, Shalom. "In This Time of War, I Propose We Give Up God." https://www.nytimes.com/2022/04/15/opinion/passover-giving-up-god.html?smid=url-share.
Augustine. *On Christian Doctrine.* Translated by D. W. Robertson, Jr. Upper Saddle River, NJ: Pearson, 1958. https://archive.org/details/onchristiandoctrooaugu_0/mode/2up.
Averroes, *The Philosophy and Theology of Averroes.* Translated by Mohammad Jamil-Ur-Rehman. Baroda: A.G. Widgery, 1921. https://www.gutenberg.org/files/65708/65708-h/65708-h.htm.
Bailey, Kenneth E. *Poet and Peasant and Through Peasant Eyes.* Grand Rapids: William B. Eerdmans, 2006.
Daube, David. "Jesus and the Samaritan Woman: The Meaning of συγχραομαι." *Journal of Biblical Literature* Vol. 69 No. 2 (June, 1950) 137-147.
Dawkins, Richard. *The Blind Watchmaker: Why the Evidence of Evolution Reveals a Universe Without Design.* New York: W. W. Norton & Co., 1986.
Dawkins, Richard. *The God Delusion.* New York: Mariner Books, Reprint edition, 2008.
Dennett, Daniel C. *Breaking the Spell: Religion as a Natural Phenomenon.* New York: Penguin, Reprint edition, 2007.
Dostoevsky, Fyodor. *The Brothers Karamazov.* Translated by Richard Pevear and Larissa Volokhonsky. New York: Picador, 1990.

Bibliography

Erickson, Millard. *Christian Theology, 3rd Edition*. Grand Rapids: Baker Academic, 2013.

Harris, Sam. "Is Religion Built upon Lies?" https://www.samharris.org/blog/item/sam-harris-vs.-andrew-sullivan. 01/16/07.

Hitchens, Christopher. *God Is Not Great: How Religion Poisons Everything*. New York: Twelve, 2009.

Hume, David. *An Enquiry Concerning Human Understanding*. Oxford: Oxford University Press, 2007.

———. *Dialogues Concerning Natural Religion*. https://www.gutenberg.org/ebooks/4583.

Keller, Phillip. *A Shepherd Looks at Psalm 23*. Grand Rapids: Zondervan, 2007.

Kern, Daniel. "The Logic of Salvation in the Gospel of John." *Philosophy and Theology* Volume 27 Number 1 (2015), 171-187.

Locke, John. *An Essay Concerning Human Understanding*. London, 1690.

Pascal, Blaise. *Pensées*. https://ccel.org/ccel/pascal/pensees/pensees.v.html.

Paley, William and Holley, Horace. *Natural Theology, Or, Evidences of the Existence and Attributes of the Deity Collected From the Appearances of Nature*. Philadelphia: John Morgan, 1802.

Plato. *The Republic*. Translated by Benjamin Jowett. London: Oxford University Press, 1892.

Tsu, Lao. *Tao Te Ching*. Translated by Gia-fu Feng and Jane English. New York: Vintage, 1974.

www.ingramcontent.com/pod-product-compliance
Lightning Source LLC
Chambersburg PA
CBHW070929160426
43193CB00011B/1627